BC | EUROPE | NEAR & MIDDLE EAST

15000 — In eastern Europe, hunters live in skin tents anchored by mammoth bones. In western Europe, cave-dwellings are in use.

In Iraq and Iran hunter-gatherers live in reed huts.
In the Near East (Anatolia and Palestine) campsites are occupied on a semi-permanent basis.
In Palestine, food gatherers and herders build round, domed huts of stone and mud.

6000

Large farming communities live in townships like Catal Hüyük in Anatolia (Turkey) and Jericho in Palestine. Houses are made from bricks of sun-dried mud. In southern Mesopotamia farming is carried on by artificial irrigation.
The development of farming in the Near East leads to the growth of permanent villages.

4000 — European farmers live in thatched long-houses made from wattle-and-daub
In Portugal and France, peoples bury their dead in tombs constructed from large stones.

Farming villages are established in the Nile valley.
Mudbrick temples are built in southern Mesopotamia.
In Egypt, unified under kings from c3100 BC, stone is used to build huge pyramids in which the bodies of Egyptian kings are buried.

2000 — In the island of Crete, seafaring traders and farmers are ruled from large, unfortified palaces.
In Britain, work on the great stone monument of Stonehenge continues over several hundred years.
Bronze-working spreads slowly westwards across Europe.

1500 — At sites in mainland Greece, Greek-speaking peoples build fortified citadels and bury the bodies of kings and aristocrats in rich graves like the Treasury of Atreus at Mycenae.

Hammurabi rules Mesopotamia from his capital, Babylon. From now on, southern Mesopotamia is known as Babylonia.
The horse-drawn chariot is introduced by peoples from the steppes of Asia. Egypt is controlled by chariot-using invaders, the Hyksos.

During a period of raids and invasions, most centres in Greece and Crete are destroyed.

The New Kingdom of Egypt becomes very powerful. Many new temples are built, especially at Luxor and Karnak.
Ironworking is carried on in Anatolia.
In Palestine, David establishes a Jewish kingdom with its capital at Jerusalem. His son, Solomon, expands the power of Israel, founding many new cities and building the Temple.
Assyrian kings build great palaces.
Nebuchadnezzar II of Babylon comes to rule all the former Assyrian possessions.

1000 — Ironworking, established in middle Europe, begins to spread westwards.
Greeks found colonies and trading stations from Spain to the Black Sea.

500 — Greece is threatened by the expanding Persian Empire. Under the leadership of Pericles, the Athenians build a magnificent new temple, the Parthenon.
Alexander the Great, leads a united Greek force in the conquest of the Persian Empire. Alexander's empire is broken up into independent Greek-ruled kingdoms.

Near East and Middle East is divided into Greek ruled kingdoms. These are eventually absorbed into the Roman empire.

AD — The Celtic peoples of Europe are ruled by chieftains based in fortified hill towns.
The Romans rise to become the strongest power in Italy. Under the emperors, Roman power extends as far as the Scottish border.

Rome's empire in the East survives the fall of the western empire. It is ruled from Constantinople (Byzantium), now a major centre of Christianity.

500 — The Vikings of Scandinavia establish colonies in Britain, Ireland, France and Sicily.

The Norman descendants of Viking conquerors seize the throne of England under William, Duke of Normandy. They control the Saxon population from fortified castles.

1000 — At places like Durham, in England, and Cluny, in France, monks supervise the building of splendid churches. There follows a great age of church building in a new style — Gothic.

Constantinople (Byzantium) is captured by Islamic Ottoman Turks, becoming the capital of the Ottoman empire.

In wealthy Tuscany there is a revival of interest in the literature, art and architecture of ancient Rome, typified by the round arch, fluted columns and the dome.

1500

FAR EAST	OTHER AREAS	BC
	In America and Australia, hunting peoples occupy cave dwellings. Hunters reach the southern tip of South America. Caves and temporary shelters are in use.	15000
		6000
In China, farmers live in villages of timber and thatch dwellings.		4000
Farming is carried on in the Indus Valley.	Farming begins in north east Mexico.	
Towns and cities grow up in the Indus Valley. At Mohenjo-Daro and Harappa, large mudbrick granaries are built to store surplus grain.	Farming villages grow up in central America.	
		2000
The Indus valley civilization disappears during a period of invasions from Iran.		
Bronze-working begins in China. The two-wheeled horse-drawn chariot is in use. The Chou dynasty of kings expand their power over a wide area.		1500
The valley of the Hwang-ho river in China is ruled by the Shang dynasty of kings, which is later displaced by the Chou dynasty. Chinese writing develops. Buddhism becomes established in India.		1000
After nearly three centuries of war between rival Chinese states, the state of Ch'in emerges victorious. The Ch'in Emperor, Shi Huang-ti, unites all China under his rule. He completes the building of the Great Wall, a defence against raids by mounted nomads of the Asian steppes.	The first ceremonial centres are built in Peru. Temples in mudbrick and stone are being built in Central and South America. The buildings are often raised on great platforms or pyramids.	500
In India, the Buddhist emperor Asoka rules a vast empire.		AD
Under the emperor Wu Ti, Chinese armies reach northern Vietnam.	The Maya people of Mexico build new temples and platforms in stone. At Teotihuacan an enormous temple city is built and enlarged over several hundred years.	
Buddhist missionaries carry the Buddhist way of life to China. Buddhist temples and pagodas are built in China.	The Toltecs create an empire in the Valley of Mexico.	500
	In Africa, the Acropolis of Zimbabwe is being built in the east. In the west, Ghana is growing into a powerful empire.	
		1000
Mongols of central Asia begin a career of conquest and invasion under the leadership of Genghis Khan, threatening Europe, Mesopotamia, India and occupying China.	The Aztecs of Mexico rule an empire from their capital at Tenochtitlan (Mexico City). Later, the Incas establish their empire in Peru.	
		1500

How they
BUILT LONG AGO

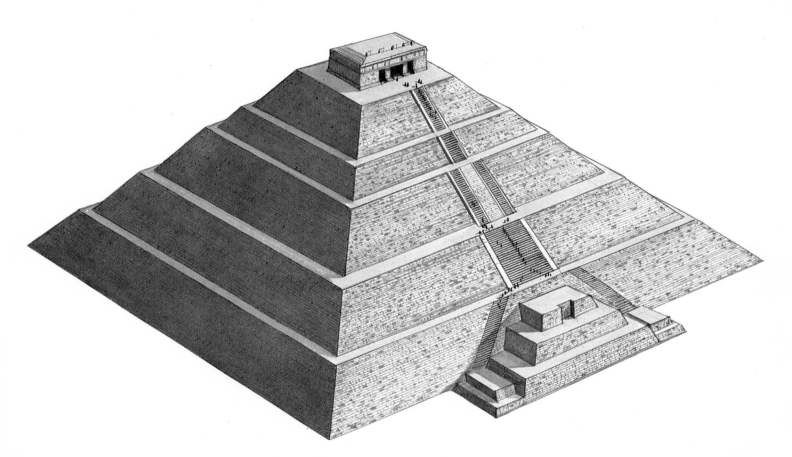

Christopher Fagg
Adrian Sington

WARWICK PRESS

Contents

Author
Christopher Fagg

Editor
Adrian Sington

Adviser
David Williams, BA

Artists
Brian and
Constance Dear
Ian Robertson
Charlotte Snook
Lindèn Artists
Temple Art

Published by Warwick Press, 730 Fifth Avenue,
New York, New York, 10019.

First published in Great Britain by Hutchinson
Junior Books Ltd. in 1981.

Copyright © 1981 Grisewood & Dempsey Ltd.

Printed in Hong Kong by Leefung-Asco
Printers Ltd.

6 5 4 3 2 1   All rights reserved.

Library of Congress Catalog No. 81-50291.

ISBN 0-531-09184-8.

The First Builders

In today's world, it is hard to think of life without powered machines. Yet the great monuments of the past, from the pyramids of Egypt to the magnificent cathedrals of the Middle Ages, were built entirely by hand, with only the most primitive machinery. In this book we look at the ways in which people built their world before the age of machines – from the earliest times to the Renaissance of the sixteenth century.

Nearly 2 million years ago, primitive man built simple windbreaks out of boulders and branches to protect themselves from the weather. Their descendants built crude wooden huts and raised animal-skin tents at stopping places along the trails made by the roaming herds of big game that they hunted.

But the building of permanent dwellings began less than 15 thousand years ago. In the Middle East, peoples who had once lived wholly by hunting began to cultivate wild grasses. These settled communities built their houses from the local materials – stone, timber and mudbrick.

Although farming did not begin in the lowlands of the Middle East, in the valleys of Egypt and Mesopotamia the Farming Revolution made great strides. Regular harvests from the fertile soil made these kingdoms rich. For the first time, people began to build large ceremonial buildings to honour their gods.

Since that time, around 6,000 years ago, people have measured the greatness of a civilization by the size and splendour of its buildings.

In East Africa, nearly 2 million years ago, distant ancestors of human beings built screens of boulders and branches. This reconstruction, based on discoveries made at Lake Turkana, Kenya, shows a group of *Australopithecus robustus* (left) peering timidly at a settlement of creatures known as '1470' hominids. '1470' had a superior intelligence which enabled them to build shelters made from boulders and branches.

Principles of Building

Hut or tent of animal hide, anchored with mammoth bones, from Siberia, 20,000 BC.

Post and lintel construction: long-house at Köln-Lindenthal, Germany, 5000–3000 BC.

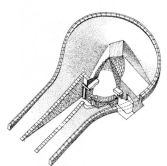

Corbelled vault: royal grave (Treasury of Atreus) at Mycenae, Greece, c1500 BC.

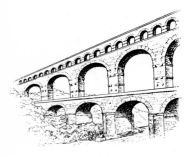

Above: Arcading; the Pont du Gard, a Roman aqueduct at Nîmes, France, c19 BC.

Right: A Roman groin vault. An intersection of two tunnel vaults.

Any structure built by human hands – from a hut to a cathedral – has to withstand certain forces, the greatest of which is gravity. Unless the structure can support its own weight it will fall to the ground.

Today architects and engineers know how to calculate scientifically the effects of forces upon structures and materials. But the builders of the past lacked this knowledge. They relied on traditional methods and techniques developed over many generations of trial and error. Because of this, changes in building methods took place very slowly.

Some 300,000 years ago, hunting peoples in Europe were building simple wooden huts. They were made of wooden stakes, bent over and lashed to form a roof. The roof was supported by central posts.

Post and Lintel

In thickly forested Europe from before 5000 BC, farmers built their timber long houses using the post and lintel method. Vertical wooden posts sunk into the ground, supported horizontal beams, or lintels. This framework was strengthened with light woven branches (wattle) coated with daub or clay. Post and lintel construction, using stone as well as timber was the main method of support until the Romans developed the arched vault.

In Mesopotamia, timber and stone were scarce. The main building material was mud. River mud mixed with straw was moulded into bricks and allowed to dry in the sun. Structures built of mudbrick had to have thick walls to carry the weight of the building. Wherever there were openings for windows or doorways the wall was weakened. At these weak points the walls were thickened. This is the simplest form of what is called *buttressing*.

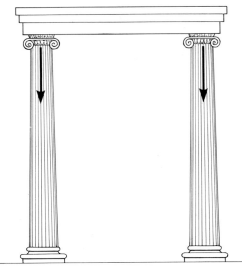

In post and lintel construction, the weight or load of the horizontal lintel is supported by vertical posts.

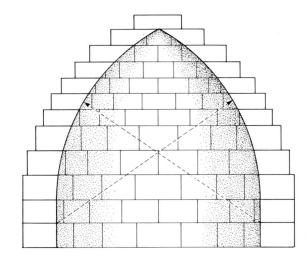

Above: A corbelled vault: Each layer, or *course*, of blocks is laid so as to overhang the course beneath. Finally the projecting corners (corbels) of the blocks are smoothed off to make an even inner surface.

Below: The round arch. The wedge-shaped stones of the arch are called voussoirs, while the central voussoir is the keystone. The arrows show the tendency of the round arch to thrust outwards.

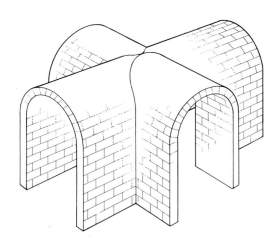

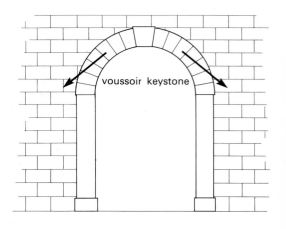

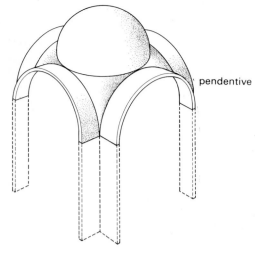

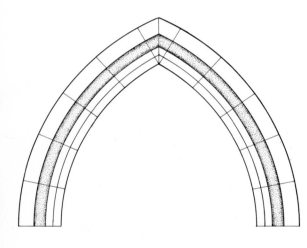

pendentive

Above: Dome construction. In Constantinople (Byzantium), architects of the 6th century AD discovered how to support a circular dome on curving triangular pieces called pendentives.

Below: The pointed arch became the basis of Gothic architecture.

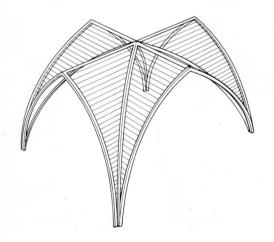

Below: A Gothic ribbed vault. The ribs carry the whole load of the vault. The spaces between them could be filled with decorative, non-structural work.

Arches and Vaults

The Roman arch could span greater distances, using less material than the post and lintel method.

In brick or stone an arch is built up of wedge-shaped pieces called *voussoirs*. Arches had been used in Mesopotamia and Egypt, but the Romans were the first to use arches on the grand scale. They discovered that the weight of the arch tends to splay the feet outwards, so that the bases of a single arch had to be very thick. On the other hand an arcade – a series of arches – need only be buttressed at each end. The Romans used this principle in aqueducts.

An arch that is extended backwards or forwards is called a vault. The Roman arched or *barrel* vault had the same problem with buttressing pierced walls that the Mesopotamians had had. The Romans realised that if they intersected two barrel vaults at right angles (called a *groin* vault) not only did it create more space but it only needed buttressing where the two vaults crossed.

In the 13th century the Crusaders imported into Europe the Middle Eastern pointed arch. This replaced the Roman arch which had severe limitations for the architects and was extremely bulky. Builders found that the pointed arched vault allowed them to intersect two vaults of different widths. Moreover it was possible to build a skeleton framework of joined arches, impossible with the Roman method. Soon church builders developed a way of transmitting the weight of a vault through arched struts, *flying buttresses*, to massive free-standing pillars outside the building. With this development the walls which no longer needed to be so thick could be pierced with great stained glass windows and have delicate arcades.

The Dome

The dome is a continuous series of arches passing through the same centre. Originally domes were formed by *corbelling* – a method by which stone blocks or bricks were laid so that each layer or *course* projected beyond the one immediately below until they met at the apex. The projecting edges were then chipped away to leave a smooth interior surface.

The Romans turned the dome into a major architectural feature and solved the old problem of thick walls by lightening the dome as much as possible. They used hollow brick ribs and further lightened it by gouging out square hollows or *coffers* from the interior surface of the dome.

Early domes were supported by continuous circular walls, which made domes hard to build into square or rectangular buildings. Byzantine architects achieved this by raising the dome above the supporting walls using piers or *pendentives*.

In the late Middle Ages, Italy saw a great revival of interest in the art and architecture of ancient Rome and Greece, magnificently achieved by Renaissance architects such as Brunelleschi, Bramante and Michelangelo.

Above: Domes. Brunelleschi's great dome for Florence Cathedral in 1470 was then the largest to be built in Europe since the fall of the Roman empire.

Above: A Gothic flying buttress. By taking the main load of the building, flying buttresses enabled walls to be pierced with large windows.

Below: The facade at Rheims cathedral completed in 1481. This cathedral proclaims the skill of High Gothic master-masons, making a suitable coronation cathedral for the kings of France.

The Mammoth Hunters

The earliest known traces of modern man – our direct ancestors – show them to be about 40,000 years old and hunters.

Today these sites are often sunny and warm. But in the days of the Palaeolithic hunters most of Europe and Western Asia had the sort of climate that is found today only in the Arctic lands of the far north. It was to last until about 12,000 BC.

Early man adapted themselves to these conditions well. They were skilled hunters with weapons of flint and bone. They lived close to forests of Scots Pine trees, which they chopped down and used for their tools and shelters. Their tools were efficient and made from wood with stone cutting edges. Mammoth ivory was occasionally used for lances as well as for sewing needles. Perhaps most important of all, they had the ability to make fire. When possible they lived in rock shelters and caves. But they were quite capable of building weatherproof, tent-like shelters of their own.

An encampment of hunters in eastern Europe, nearly 25,000 years ago. They live by hunting mammoths and wild horses. Their sturdy tents of animal hides are weighted down with mammoth tusks and bones. Each has a hearth in a bowl-shaped hollow.

Here we see an encampment at Pushkari in South Russia about 25,000 years ago. Groups similar to this were scattered over an enormous area, from south-western Europe to Central and Eastern Asia.

This community made its living from hunting and perhaps its most important quarry was the mammoth – a shaggy-coated member of the elephant family, standing three metres at the shoulder and now extinct. The traces of mammoth bones found near the buildings suggest that mammoth meat formed a large part of the local diet. One woman of the community was carefully buried, at her death, with two great bones – the shoulder blades of a mammoth – to cover her body. The remains of mammoths also played a valuable part in the construction of buildings. Their hides were used to make tunics and trousers not unlike Eskimo costume.

The hunters lived in tents made of animal skins sewn together and stretched over a wooden framework. They were anchored at ground level with the huge bones and tusks of mammoths. Tents like these could be easily dismantled and the skins transported to new campsites as the hunters followed the seasonal migrations of mammoth, reindeer and bison. Sometimes these migrations meant the hunters

and their families travelling very long distances. In many ways this way of life is like that of the American Plains Indians, who until the 19th century lived by hunting wild bison. Indian *tipis*, too, were made of animal hides stretched across a wooden framework.

On the way the hunters would shelter in caves. Cave life, however, had its dangers. Large rocks frequently fell from the roof crushing the inhabitants. There was also no retreat if suddenly confronted by a lion or bear.

Other remains have been found at a place called Dolní Věstonice in Czechoslovakia. There, huts were built on sloping ground so as to be sheltered by the crest of the hill. Floors were hollowed out so that people would be protected against the wind while they were sleeping. One floor was even covered with small pieces of limestone. These prevented the floor from being trampled into mud, and from being worn into irregular hollows where the traffic of feet was heaviest.

Another hut was roughly circular and about six metres in diameter. It was surrounded by a low wall of clay mixed with pieces of limestone. Upright posts, driven into the wall, supported the roof. At their base they were reinforced with large stones. The roof was sloped in order to let the rain

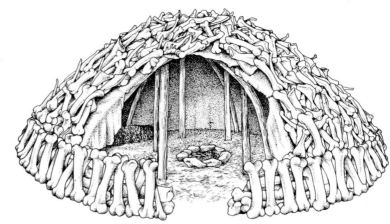

run off and was probably made of branches, grass, earth and animal skins – weighted down with mammoth bones. The hearth was the sacred centre of the tent. Fire was a vital possession to be worshipped and cherished by these hunters.

All these finds show that the basic principles of building were well established. Sites were carefully chosen for maximum protection from the weather and in places where water could run off easily. Shelters were firmly supported both inside and out by a wooden frame made with trees taken from the local pine forests.

Above: Where timber was scarce, hunters made the framework of their dwellings from large mammoth bones, as in this oval hut discovered at Mezhirich in Russia. At another Russian site, the remains of huts up to 30 metres long have been found, their floors hollowed out below ground level as extra protection from arctic winds.

First Farmers

During the Ice Age, building skills were limited by the harsh environment. Raw materials were scarce and there was a constant need to keep moving in search of food. The greatest advances were in weapons for hunting, and the knives, scrapers and other tools needed to butcher carcasses and prepare hides for clothing and shelter. In about 12,000 BC, however the climate began to grow warmer. Forests crept northwards across Europe. Wild wheat and barley began to grow in the high mountain valleys of the Near East. Here people first turned from hunting to harvesting them. Soon they were sowing the seeds of the wild grains in cultivated ground. Regular harvests allowed them to live permanently in the same place in settled communities. Gradually, farming ways of life spread into Europe.

The first European farmers were frontiersmen, clearing virgin forest to plant wheat, barley, peas, beans and lentils. They also kept pigs, cattle and sheep in large pens.

Early European farmers build wattle-and-daub longhouses at a site they have cleared from the forest. On the left the wattle is being fitted prior to being daubed. When complete, the village will be made up of five or six large houses. The man on the left is eating river oysters, while the women on the right are crushing ochre for paint and grain for bread.

This is a well-established farming community in Central Europe in 5000 or 4000 BC. The task of building the village is shared by everybody. These people are building sturdy longhouses using the raw materials that they can easily get hold of locally. In this case they are flint, which they dig up from the ground and use for making tools, wood for the main structure of the houses, and clay – which, mixed with straw and animal dung, is used as a weatherproof plaster for outside walls.

The chief building tool was the polished stone axe, used both to fell trees and to trim timbers to shape. The axe head was shaped so as to fit easily into a wooden handle, and its highly polished and sharpened face enabled it to bite deeply into the wood. The cutting edge was kept sharp by grinding it on a sandstone block. The best materials for axes were flint and certain types of hard, finely grained rock.

Wattle and Daub

The type of longhouses being built are up to 20 metres in length. Settlements grew up near lakes and rivers, and these provided the clay for building. After clearing and levelling the site, upright posts were set into the ground, so as to support a framework of beams and rafters. The

timbers were firmly fixed together by jointing – fitting the end of one piece into a hole cut in the other – reinforced by lashing with cord (made from animal wool) or rawhide (made from thin strips of hide). The spaces between the uprights were filled with wattle – split twigs or branches woven over thin stakes. It is probable that certain trees were pollarded – deliberately cut back – to encourage the growth of long, straight twigs for this purpose.

Roofs in Europe had to be sloping to allow rain or melting snow to run off easily. They were covered with overlapping layers of straw or reed thatch fixed to a wattle base.

A man is hard at work applying a thick layer of plaster to the outside of a nearly completed house. The plaster was made of clay puddled with water to a smooth consistency. Chopped straw and animal dung were added to the mixture in order to prevent the plaster shrinking, and thus cracking, as it dried on the wall.

Longhouses like these were built in Europe for well over a thousand years. They may have housed clans, or groups of families, or they may have been the home of a single family along with their animals, stores and produce. Later, the pattern changed, and houses became smaller. But the basic method of building – timber, thatch, wattle and daub – remained until the Roman conquest of western Europe and on into the medieval period.

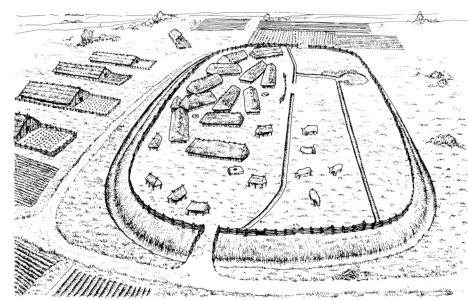

An aerial view of a European farming village, 5000–4500 BC. The large enclosure contains byres and sties for cattle and pigs. Peas, beans and lentils are growing in the vegetable patches in front of the houses. Villages of up to 50 dwellings are known to have existed. Over a long period, farming and grazing by animals gradually exhausted the land, making it necessary to move on to new settlements.

A Stone-Age Town

At the time when farming was just beginning in Europe, 6000 BC, sizeable settlements already existed in the Near East, for this is where farming first began to develop, perhaps from 9000 BC. In the mountains of Anatolia (Turkey), the Iranian, Syrian and Palestinian people developed new types of cultured wheat and barley from wild varieties. They also domesticated the wild sheep, goat and pig which lived there. Areas of settlement were linked by trade which probably helped the spread of farming skills. Obsidian, the best material for tools and weapons, was a valuable trade item. There were skilled craftsmen — weavers, potters and makers of fine stone tools, weapons and even luxuries such as mirrors of polished obsidian.

In places like Çatal Hüyük and Hacilar in Anatolia, and Jericho in Palestine, villages grew into large townships housing thousands of people. In 6000 BC Çatal Hüyük was a thriving town on a low mound in a valley near the Carsamba river in the heart of a fertile plain.

At first sight, Çatal Hüyük would look rather like a Near Eastern village today, a collection of flat-roofed, mudwalled houses. But on closer inspection we would start to see some strange features.

To begin with there are no streets. The houses are built back to back and side by side. Occasionally an open house plot is used as a courtyard. To get from one part of the town to another, you have to walk across the roofs, climbing from level to level up and down wooden ladders. The houses, too, are rather odd. They have no doorways. Instead, each house has a hole in the roof from which a ladder descends to the interior.

There are at least 1000 of these houses. Each house is rectangular, about 6 metres by 4 metres and about 4 metres high. The foundations are not in the earth, but on top of the crumbling remains of the previous house, which gives the town its peculiar stepped look.

Mudbrick Furniture

The main materials the builders are using are timber and rectangular bricks made from sun-dried mud. First they build a sturdy framework of wooden posts and beams. Then they build up the walls with courses of brick, bound together with a mortar of semi-liquid mud. When the

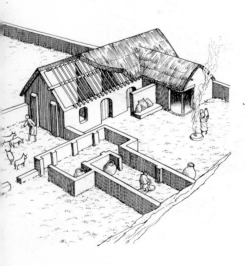

This is a rectangular mudbrick farmhouse from Hassuna in northern Mesopotamia. After 5000 BC, farming spread farther eastwards to Iran and beyond.

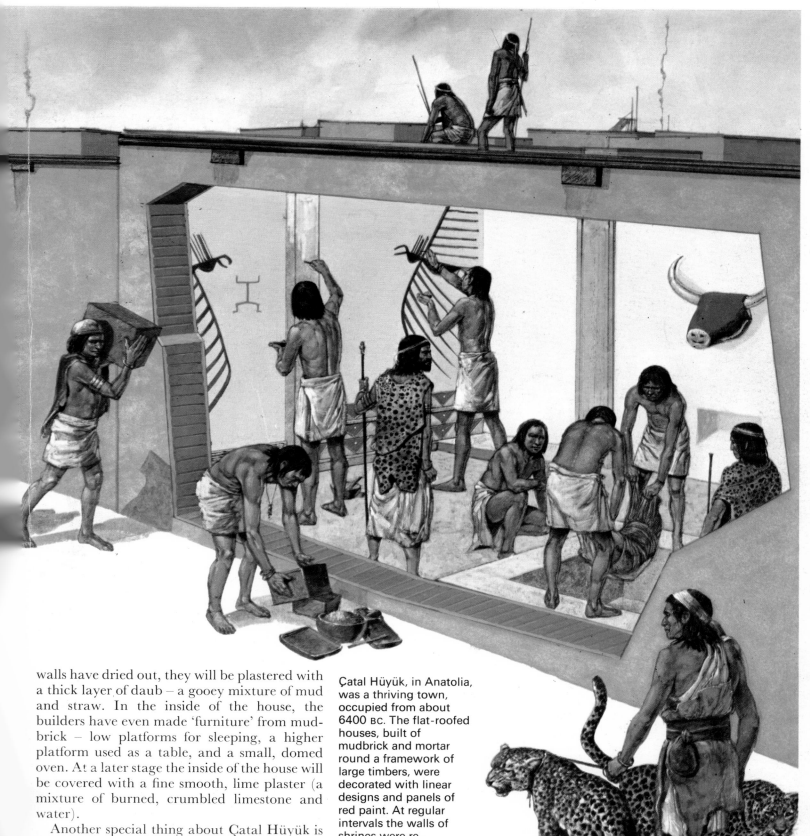

walls have dried out, they will be plastered with a thick layer of daub – a gooey mixture of mud and straw. In the inside of the house, the builders have even made 'furniture' from mud-brick – low platforms for sleeping, a higher platform used as a table, and a small, domed oven. At a later stage the inside of the house will be covered with a fine smooth, lime plaster (a mixture of burned, crumbled limestone and water).

Another special thing about Çatal Hüyük is that the people have set aside particular build-ings for some kind of religious use. The walls of these shrines will be painted with pictures of huge birds of prey. The shrines were also decorated with the skulls of bulls, carefully plastered and painted to look as lifelike as possible. Much remains mysterious about this strange town and its inhabitants. It is as though it is poised between two worlds – looking back to the wandering hunters of the past, and looking forward to an age of cities and temples, the first achievements of civilization.

Çatal Hüyük, in Anatolia, was a thriving town, occupied from about 6400 BC. The flat-roofed houses, built of mudbrick and mortar round a framework of large timbers, were decorated with linear designs and panels of red paint. At regular intervals the walls of shrines were re-plastered, and painted with headless figures and huge birds of prey: animal skulls, plastered with clay to resemble the living animal, were hung on the walls. Two men lower the remains of a human body, which has been allowed to rot, into a shallow grave beneath the living room floor. Leopards were kept as sacred pets.

First Cities

Farming and building skills first developed in the uplands of the Near East. But life there long remained at the level of the village or small town. Great advances, however, took place to the south-east – in the broad, fertile valley between the Tigris and Euphrates rivers. This land, later known as Mesopotamia, was originally the home of the Sumerians in the south. They built dams and canals to control the violent flooding of the rivers, and to water the rich soil during the scorching summers. Harvests were plentiful and populations grew. The work came to be controlled and organized by local temples, staffed by a class of priest-administrators. In time, the temples became the centres of large cities, with populations many thousands strong. With city life came the first brilliant flowering of civilization – the development of writing, mathematics, astronomy, the arts, and the building of great temples. This tradition of building temples and cities was carried on by other peoples who came to rule the region – the Akkadians and Babylonians of central Mesopotamia, and the fierce Assyrians of the north.

The Sumerians built their first large temples in about 3500 BC. The temples were built in honour of the local gods who protected the people and gave them good harvests. The god was thought of as the landlord of the temple grounds. From time to time a new 'house' was built for the god. The old temple was filled in and buried and a new one built on top of it.

The Sumerians lacked stone and timber, which had to be transported from elsewhere over long distances. Their main building material was brick, made from the unlimited supply of river mud. There were two kinds of brick: unfired mudbrick, which was dried in the sun, and burnt brick, which was fired in a kiln. Burnt brick, which was more expensive to make, was used mostly as a decorative facing to cover the basic structure of unfired mudbrick. Coloured cones of baked clay were also used to decorate the drab surface of mudbrick temples.

Vast reedbeds grew near the river, providing another important material. At a very early stage, houses and even temples were made by tying bundles of reeds together to make a frame and then covering it with layers of woven reed matting. Structures like these continued to be used as storehouses and as shelters for animals. Woven reed baskets were used to carry mud from the river to the site where the bricks were made. Reed matting and cables were laid at intervals between layers of mudbrick to stop walls from going out of shape as the mudbricks dried out and shrank.

The achievements of the Sumerian builders, using only simple materials, were based on detailed organization and administration. From early times, temple priests regulated the mass labour needed to build and maintain the dams, canals and ditches on which the harvest depended. The development of written records and accounts allowed the temples, and later kings and emperors, to plan and control huge projects – temples, palaces, fortifications, even whole cities.

Babylon, on the Euphrates, grew to become one of the most famous of Mesopotamian cities. It first became powerful as the capital of the mighty Hammurabi (1792–1750 BC) who united north and south under his rule.

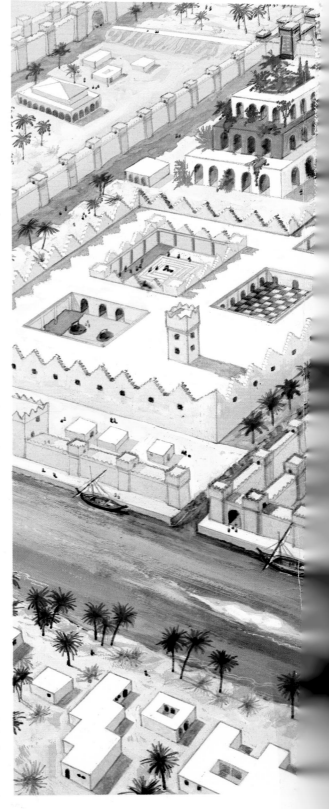

'Is not this great Babylon, that I have built for the house of the kingdom, by the might, and for the honour of my majesty?' *(Daniel 4:28–30).* When Nebuchadnezzar (605–562 BC) decided to rebuild Babylon, he was following traditions and methods already 2500 years old. Mudbrick was the main building material, faced with fired brick set in a waterproof bitumen mortar. On the left you can see the royal palace and the huge stepped tower containing the famous Hanging Gardens. A Processional way leads from the Ishtar Gate (top left) skirts the palace enclosure, and temple precinct, with its towering ziggurat and leads across the bridge over the river Euphrates.

Hammurabi established the god of Babylon, *Marduk*, as supreme ruler of the gods. From then on Babylon had a lasting influence as a religious centre. The city often fell to invaders, but even foreign kings saw it as their duty to defend Babylon and, when necessary, to rebuild it. In 689 BC, and again in 648, Babylon was sacked by Assyrian kings from the north. But the Assyrian empire fell, and Nebuchadnezzar – whose father had seized Babylon from the Assyrians – decided to rebuild the city more splendidly.

Nebuchadnezzar's Babylon

Here we see Nebuchadnezzar's Babylon. On the left is the royal palace. Nebuchadnezzar wrote: 'I laid the foundation of the new palace firmly, and built it mountain high with bitumen and baked bricks. Huge cedars I caused to be laid for its roof, door leaves of cedar mounted with copper, thresholds and hinges made of bronze I fitted to its gates …' In one of the five courtyards of the palace is a tall, stepped tower. This tower, planted with shrubs and palm trees, became famous as the *Hanging Gardens of Babylon* – one of the Seven Wonders of the ancient world. The palace is approached by a sacred processional way, the Avenue of Lions. Its mudbrick walls are covered with reliefs of fierce animals made up of thousands of glazed and coloured tiles. With its great temples to Marduk and its wide walls running 18 kilometres around the city, Babylon was described by the Greek historian Herodotus as 'surpassing in splendour any city of the known world.'

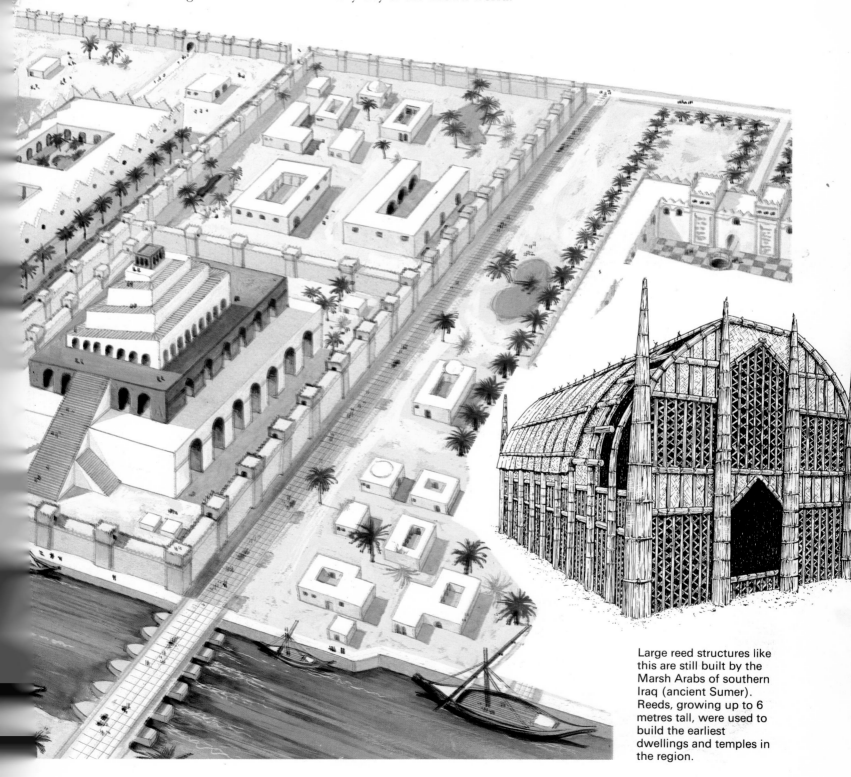

Large reed structures like this are still built by the Marsh Arabs of southern Iraq (ancient Sumer). Reeds, growing up to 6 metres tall, were used to build the earliest dwellings and temples in the region.

Monuments in the Desert

Building a pyramid. On the right hand side a group of scribes discuss the plans, drawn on scrolls made from papyrus – a reed that grows on the banks of the Nile. In the foreground, men are sharpening copper chisels for the skilled masons who are smoothing and squaring the stone blocks. Unskilled labourers – peasants from the fields – drag the blocks on wooden sledges towards the huge ramp built along side the unfinished pyramid. More than 2,300,000 blocks of stone were used in the Great Pyramid of Khufu (Cheops).

Egyptian civilization, like that of Sumer, was based on the intensive cultivation of a fertile river valley. Each year, until modern times, the river Nile flooded between June and October. The floods left a deposit of rich silt – the famous 'black earth' – on each bank. For about 800 kilometres this fertile strip, known as the Cultivation, is no wider than 12 kilometres. But in the north it fans out into a wide, triangular area, known as the Delta where the Nile subdivides into different channels and flows into the Mediterranean. East and west of the Cultivation stretch parched, empty deserts with occasional oases. The ancient Egyptians always thought of the Nile valley as two lands – Lower Egypt around the Delta, and Upper Egypt to the south. About 3100 BC a king called Menes united them. From then on, dynasties of kings (the Pharaohs) ruled Egypt until it was conquered by the Romans. Protected by deserts and the Mediterranean Sea, its kings, wealthy and secure, filled the Nile Valley with magnificent stone temples and monuments.

About 2600 BC an Egyptian king called Khufu ordered a magnificent tomb to be built for a very important person – himself. It may seem strange to order your own tomb, but the Egyptians were very concerned with the life that they believed awaited a person after death. They thought that the spirit, or soul, of a dead person lived on as long as the earthly body survived. Accordingly, they tried to make the dead body last as long as possible. The king was the most important man in the state. When he died, his body was carefully dried and preserved with salts and spices. This process, called *mummification*, lasted as long as 70 days. At the end of that time, the king's body was buried, together with his richest and most important possessions, which he believed that he would take with him to the Next World. Since his body was to last forever, it followed that his tomb, too, must survive. King Khufu may get his wish: his tomb, the Great Pyramid, still stands today, 4500 years later.

Khufu's Great Pyramid

The work of building Khufu's Great Pyramid went on for more than 30 years, and occupied many thousands of workers – from skilled craftsmen to unskilled labourers. This was possible only because the king was thought of as a god, 'the father and mother of all men'. He owned the land and the people and no-one questioned his authority.

Building was in the hands of the king's *vizier* or chief minister. With a staff of scribes, the *vizier* selected the site and gathered together the skilled workers – surveyors, stonecutters, masons, mortar makers – that he needed. He arranged for limestone and granite blocks to be cut in the quarries and transported them down river by boat. The progress of the work had to be planned carefully. The thousands of unskilled

workers, who provided the musclepower for heavy work, could only be spared for part of each year.

The site was in the desert, beyond the fertile land on the west bank of the Nile. A great square was marked out so that its sides, 230 metres long, faced north, south, east and west. The problem was levelling the site. The Egyptians devised an ingenious solution. A network of linked trenches were dug. Water was poured into them. At the water line a mark was made. This was done along all the trench walls. Finally gangs of workers chipped away the rocky ground down to the line, using nothing but other lumps of rock.

Next, work began on a tunnel which, when completed would lead to a burial chamber dug out of the rock some five metres below ground level. Men used mallets made of a very hard stone called *dolerite*. They smashed their way into the bedrock. Behind them, other workers smoothed and squared off the rough walls of the tunnel with copper chisels.

Meanwhile, huge blocks of limestone and granite were arriving by boat from the quarries. They weighed up to 15 tons each, and had to be manhandled from quarry to boat, and from boat to the site, on great wooden sleds. More than 2,000,000 blocks would be needed to build the pyramid. Each block had to be chiselled and smoothed until its top and ends were perfectly square.

The blocks were hauled up ramps of earth and levered into position on wooden rollers. Skilled stonemasons supervised the exact placing of each block in a thin bed of mortar. This was a mixture of sand, lime and water. Besides being used as a fixative, it was also used as a lubricant when pulling the great blocks of stone up the earthramps. As the pyramid grew, the earth ramps wound ever higher around its sides.

Finally, the earth ramps could be shovelled away. After many years of toil, the Great Pyramid was finally completed. Standing 166 metres high, it is still the largest structure ever built.

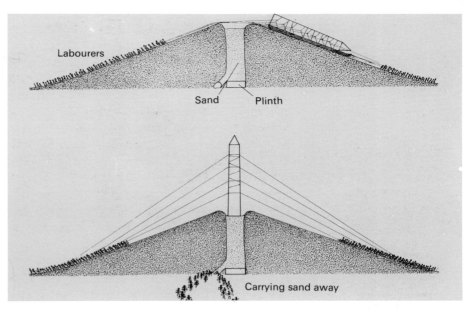

Above: Setting up an obelisk, a tall inscribed stone monument. The obelisk was dragged on a wooden sled up an artificial ramp surrounding a funnel filled with sand. At the base of the funnel was the plinth on which the obelisk would stand. The obelisk was hauled into an upright position on top of the sand, which was gradually removed through a tunnel at ground level. As the sand sank, the obelisk settled until it rested on its plinth. Finally the ramp itself was removed.

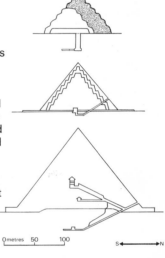

Right: The development of pyramid building. From top to bottom: Early mudbrick tomb covering a royal burial chamber (c3000 BC). Mudbrick tomb built up in stages and enlarged to form a step pyramid, cased in limestone (c2686 BC). Step pyramid enlarged and given a smooth casing of stone blocks (c2600 BC). True pyramid, that of King Khufu (Cheops), who reigned c2590–67 BC. More than 30 royal pyramids exist in Egypt, together with some 60 others in what is now Sudan.

Building a House in Egypt

As we have seen, the Egyptians were skilled builders in stone. Egypt had excellent sources of high quality limestone, sandstone, alabaster and granite. But the task of quarrying and transporting stone required skill and enormous labour. Only state buildings, such as royal tombs and temples were built entirely of stone. For the rest the Egyptians, like the Sumerians, used unfired mudbrick. Even in the mansions of the nobility, stone was used only for door lintels, thresholds and for the bases of supporting pillars. Mudbrick was very suitable as a building material in the very dry conditions of the Egyptian desert. There was nothing to destroy them except the wind blown sand and this was avoided by plastering the walls with mud, and building them at an angle to the prevailing wind.

The design of Egyptian houses was influenced by the need to keep them cool during the scorching heat of summer. The windows were very small to keep out the sunlight, and the doorways faced north to take advantage of Egypt's prevailing breeze, which blows from north to south. The outside walls were whitewashed which had the effect – whether the Egyptians knew it or not – of reflecting the sun's fierce heat.

Most houses had an entrance lobby, just inside the door, leading to a cool inner room. From here a stairway led up to a flat roof, where Egyptian families liked to sit out in the cool of the evening under a shelter of reed matting. Even in workmen's houses the inner walls were often colour-washed and painted with human figures and plant designs. The houses of the rich were larger and more spacious, with extra rooms for the family and the household servants. In towns like Thebes, where land was scarce, a rich man's house might be two or even three storeys high. But, where space allowed, mansions were built on one level around a series of shady courtyards, and surrounded by gardens with pools of fish, exotic plants and beautifully painted murals.

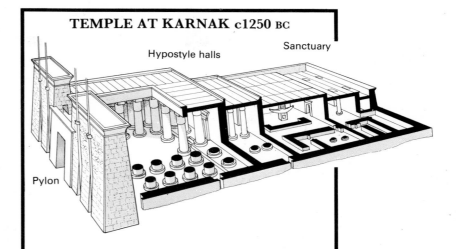

Hypostyle halls

Sanctuary

Pylon

The main temple of Amun at Karnak is a typical example of fine Egyptian temple building. The main gateway, with its two tall towers, or *pylons*, led through to pillared courtyards and on to an inner shrine where the statue of the god stood. The capitals of the heavy stone pillars were shaped after Egyptian trees and plants – the date palm, the papyrus reed and the lotus flower. The god Amun came to be the most powerful of the Egyptian gods: at one point Amun 'owned' 700,000 acres of land, 65 cities and towns and more than 86,000 workers. These vast resources provided the wealth and the manpower to build great temple centres at Karnak and Luxor devoted to his worship. The workers who laboured on these projects were divided into two classes: the peasants who undertook heavy, unskilled work, and the skilled craftsmen – carvers, painters, sculptors and goldsmiths – who did the detailed finishing work. The peasants worked during the season when the fields were flooded by the Nile. They were paid in food and provisions. The craftsmen, who lived in their own specially built townships, received food and supplies, together with clothing, tools and equipment for their work.

Making Bricks

Here you can see men hard at work building new houses at the edge of town. Some men fetch water in large clay jars, while others mix up water and clay to the right consistency for the brick moulds, using hoes and their feet. The rather pebbly mixture is strengthened with chopped straw. Two brickmakers are 'striking' the bricks – turning the mixture out of wooden moulds onto level ground – where the bricks will dry for two or three days in the sun before being used. The bricks are quite large, about $23 \times 11 \times 8$ cms for houses and larger, up to $38 \times 16 \times 16$ cms for palaces and forts, although the dimensions vary from area to area.

Building Walls

They are laid in courses two bricks wide with mortar between each course. To prevent the wall warping when the mudbricks shrink as they dry, an occasional air-space is left and in larger buildings a large piece of cedar wood serves to 'tie' the bricks. So successful were the Egyptian bricklayers that some mudbrick walls, built nearly 4000 years ago, survive to this day.

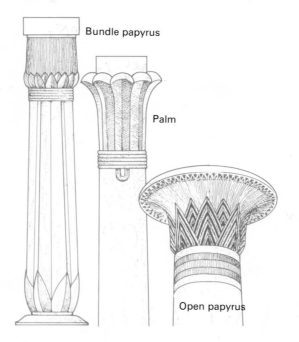

Bundle papyrus

Palm

Open papyrus

The stone pillars of Egyptian temples were carved in the shape of plants and trees because the pillared courtyard, or *hypostyle*, of the temple symbolised in Egyptian myth, the first land to emerge from the waters which once covered the Earth. The most common stylised forms were derived from the two commonest plants in Egypt – papyrus and palm.

Birthplace of the Gods

In the New World, civilization first developed in central America – Mexico and Guatemala. The Indian peoples who lived there were descendants of early hunters who had entered North America 40,000 years ago, when it was still linked to Asia. By 1500 BC the Indians of central Mexico were skilled farmers of maize (sweetcorn), beans, squashes (such as pumpkin), tomatoes and other food crops. In about 1100 BC, these people began to build shrines raised on clay platforms or mounds: the shrines were no more than altars protected by thatched roofs. From about 300 BC, stone temple-pyramids were built, surrounded by great platforms, plazas and ceremonial buildings. At the same time, the Indians made great advances in compiling extremely accurate calendars based on mathematics and astronomy, which they recorded in a type of writing. Their way of life was dominated by the worship of many gods.

One of the first great centres to be built was at Teotihuacán, about 40 kilometres northeast of Mexico City. Teotihuacán was in a valley which commanded a route to valuable deposits of green obsidian, prized for tools and weapons. The name means 'birthplace of the gods'. According to the legend, the gods gathered there to decide who should carry the burden of the Sun. Two gods came forward, the wealthy Tecuaztecatl, in his rich clothing, and the poor, ragged Nanahuatzin, dressed in paper. To become the Sun, one of them would have to jump into a roaring fire. When it came to it, Tecuaztecatl hesitated – but Nanahuatzin leaped straight into the flames. Ashamed of his cowardice, Tecuaztecatl also hurled himself into the fire. He became the Moon.

The earliest shrine at Teotihuacán was a cave, over which a clay pyramid was built, surmounted by a primitive temple or altar. But as the farming population of the area grew wealthier, they rebuilt the temple-pyramid in stone. We do not know how the work was organized. It may have been that people saw it as a religious duty. Alternatively, a group of priest-chieftains, under a ruling sovereign, may have extorted forced labour from serfs or captives. In any case, the work was carried out with great skill.

Pyramid of the Sun

The completed Pyramid of the Sun was 225 metres wide and some 75 metres high. Its main face points towards the precise point on the horizon at which the Sun sets over Teotihuacán on the day it reaches its highest point in the sky – the summer solstice. It is built of clay, faced with limestone blocks, jointed with lime mortar.

Since the people of central America did not have metal tools, the achievement is all the greater. The stone must have been quarried and dressed – squared – with stone tools. One way of quarrying was to drive wooden wedges into natural faults in the rock, and soak the wood. As the wedges expanded they cracked a section of the rock away from its natural bed. The stone was dressed by pounding it with mallets or mauls of harder stones. It was then smoothed by rubbing with an abrasive, such as sand, using another piece of stone as a smoother. The blocks would have had to be hauled to the site by hand, since the people had no draught animals, and the wheel was unknown.

The most luxurious dwellings in Teotihuacán were the palaces of the inner circle of priest-chieftains. They were of adobe brick – made from sundried mud – plastered with a lime stucco washed with pink or green. The floors, too, were plaster: they were whitewashed and burnished with pebbles and smooth stones to a silvery shine. The walls were covered in rich paintings in colours made from various earths and rocks ground into powder.

Teotihuacán's greatness came to a sudden end in about AD 900, when it was destroyed and abandoned. But centres like it continued to be built in other parts of central and South America until the Spanish invasion in the 16th century.

The pyramids of the Sun (right) and the Moon (left) at Teotihuacan, Mexico. The scale and grandeur of the Mayan ceremonial architecture contrasts with the desolate scrubland that surrounds it.

One type of Mayan construction: rough stonework finished with a layer of stucco.

The Stonehenge Mystery

On Salisbury Plain in southern England lies one of the most impressive and mysterious of all pre-historic structures – Stonehenge. It seems to have been built in several stages, between 3000 and 1500 BC. Little is known about the people who built it. But this one great structure shows us that they had remarkable intelligence and organization.

Archaeologists used to believe that Stonehenge was designed to contain the graves of important men, and perhaps for worshipping the spirits of the dead. But, recently, some scientists have claimed that it was built as a primitive observatory to predict the movement of the Sun and Moon.

Originally, Stonehenge was a circle of pits cut into the chalk rock with some standing stones. The whole structure was surrounded by a circular bank and ditch. Over 700 years later a horseshoe of stones was erected. Geologists have discovered that the bluestones the builders used were brought from the Preseli Mountains in South Wales more than 300 kilometres away.

Later, perhaps several centuries later, came the great sarsen stones which were to form the outer circle of Stonehenge; the bluestones were re-arranged inside. Sarsen is an intensely hard form of sandstone, far tougher than granite. Blocks weighing up to 40 tons were brought from the Marlborough Downs, a distance of 30 kilometres. They must have been dragged on wooden rollers or sledges. The next stage was the enormously difficult task of dressing the huge blocks and hoisting them into position. We can see how this was done using large numbers of men to manhandle the huge blocks.

The Rising Sun

It has long been known that the inner horseshoe of Stonehenge lines up with a point on the horizon very close to where the Sun rises on Midsummer Day. Since then, two other stones have been shown to point where, 4000 years ago, the Moon could be seen setting in its most northerly position. (Since then the Earth's position relative to the Sun and Moon has changed slightly.) Many other imaginery lines have been drawn through important points at Stonehenge, which seem to match up with particular positions of the Sun and Moon through the year.

It may have been that the builders of Stonehenge performed sacrifices to the Sun and Moon on the exact days when they changed their course in the heavens. Did people feel that these were the times when the gods of the Sun and Moon were most likely to withdraw their light, putting the harvest in jeopardy, unless they received a special sacrifice? Sadly we may never know the answer.

We do know, however, that vast human effort was spent in building Stonehenge, requiring a large and efficient organization.

Hundreds of men are needed to drag the huge sarsen stones which have arrived by river on rafts. The cross stones are lifted onto increasingly higher platforms until finally they rest on the standing stones. The method of jointing is a direct link with timber construction.

Left: Megaliths ('great stones') were built by communities on the Atlantic coasts of Europe from about 4000 BC. This megalithic tomb is from Portugal.

The Age of Metals

For thousands of years people made their tools and weapons from different kinds of stone. But between 4000 and 3000 BC true metalworking first developed in the Near East and Anatolia. It was a long time before mass production of metal implements was to be possible, so that traditional methods of stoneworking continued even in metal-producing areas. But the Age of Metals had dawned.

The earliest known man-made metal objects were found at Çayönü Tepesi in south east Anatolia. They are made of copper and include three pins, a small tablet and the point of a reamer (a tool for enlarging or boring holes). Experts think that they were made in about 7000 BC. Objects such as these would have been made by hammering out surface nuggets of almost pure copper washed down by rivers from rich mountain deposits.

A 150-metre deep copper mine near Salzburg in eastern Austria about 1200 BC. In northern Europe, the secrets of bronze working were not known until after 1500 BC, about the same time as bronze working first began in China. Inset: Miners dig tunnels by lighting a fire against the rock face: when the rock is hot, they throw cold water onto it to make it split. The miners use bronze picks to clear the debris. As the tunnel grows deeper, the miners have to cut stout timbers to support the roof; notched ladders connect one level with another. Lighting is provided by torches made from bundles of twigs. The ore, transported to the surface in leather sacks, is crushed by men with heavy stone hammers. Then a worker washes the crushed ore in the water from a diverted stream, to separate it from non-metalbearing rock. The shiny concentrated ore is carried down the mountain to smelting furnaces from which ingots of pure copper will emerge. The surrounding pine forests provide pit-props and fuel for the mining operations.

True metalworking, however, involves separating the pure metal from the rocks (ore) which contain it, by heating. At a particular point the metal becomes liquid. This point – the melting point – occurs at different temperatures for different metals. Copper, for example, melts at a temperature of 700°–800° Centigrade. The process of heating ore to extract the metal is called *smelting*.

Liquid metal can be cast by pouring the molten copper into pre-shaped moulds. On cooling, the metal becomes solid. The earliest moulds were pieces of stone in which the shape had been hollowed out. Later moulds were made in two pieces, clamped together so that both sides of the object were shaped identically.

The first copper tools were probably less efficient than their stone equivalents. Copper is rather a soft metal and needs frequent re-heating and hammering to maintain its edge. However copper had two advantages over stone. It took less time to produce a copper implement; and if a stone axe broke, it had to be discarded, but a broken copper axe could be melted down and re-cast to make a new one very quickly.

Bronze

By 3000 BC the coppersmiths of the Near East had discovered that, by adding small proportions of another metal, tin, to copper, they produced a harder metal. This mixture, or *alloy*, of copper and tin is called bronze. It could be cast easily, and its hardness made it far more suitable for tools and weapons than pure copper. But tin was very rare which made bronze expensive to make. In the cities of Sumer, for example, only the very wealthy possessed bronze implements.

Iron

Bronze-working was firmly established in the Near East soon after 3000 BC. But nearly 1500 years were to pass before the problem of ironworking was mastered by the Hittites of Anatolia. Iron occurred more commonly than copper and tin. However, it was mixed with impurities which made it difficult to extract from its ore, and its melting point was too high for it to be cast like copper and bronze. The iron ore had first to be roasted in a slow fire with charcoal to remove the sulphur – the main impurity. It was then heated in a furnace until it formed a red-hot spongy mass called the *bloom* which still contained impurities or *slag*. The 'smith' then hammered the red-hot bloom on an anvil, while the slag flew off in sparks. It was then ready to be hammered into shape.

METALWORK IN CHINA

Bronze production began independently in China under the Sh'ang Dynasty of kings (1500–1027 BC). It grew out of the methods the Chinese had developed for firing pottery at high temperatures (about 1200°C, 300°C higher than the furnaces of the Near East could reach). By the 5th century BC, the Chinese had furnaces capable of melting iron. It was not until 1500 AD that Europe devised a way to melt iron, 2000 years later.

Below: Ingots of copper, imported by the islanders of Crete from Cyprus in 2000 BC. The protruding bits were presumably to make them easier to handle.

Frescoes of Minos

Above: Decorating the walls of one of the state apartments in the palace at Knossos, c1700 BC. A young priestess wearing her tight-fitting bodice and pleated skirt looks on impatiently.

Right: The Palace at Knossos, Crete in 1700 BC. Good stone and strong timber make the palace resilient to the frequent earthquakes. Public rooms were on the second floor. The royal apartments, storerooms and shrines were built around a central court.

Some time around 6000 BC, Anatolians began to colonize the uninhabited islands of the Aegean. The largest of these was the island of Crete, with its fertile valleys, plains and thickly forested mountains, abounding with wild game. Safe from invaders, the Cretans developed a rich way of life based on farming, stockbreeding and the cultivation of the olive. From early times, Cretan craftsmen produced exquisitely engraved gemstones, fine painted pottery and, later, beautiful metal objects in gold, silver and bronze. The seafaring Cretans traded their products with the peoples of the Aegean, Anatolia, the Levant and Egypt. After 2000 BC, this trade seems to have been regulated and organized from palaces like those at Knossos, Phaistos and Mallia. The palaces were complexes of religious shrines, state apartments, granaries, storehouses and craft workshops, surrounded by cities of stone houses laid out in streets and squares. In later Greek legend, Crete was ruled by King Minos. His name has given us the word 'Minoan', used to describe the brilliant and exuberant Cretan civilization of this period.

Much of what we know about the life of the ancient Minoans comes from the lively, uninhibited scenes with which they decorated the walls of their houses and palaces. Some pictures show the rich natural life of Crete and its coastal waters: birds amid sprays of leaves and flowers, a deer leaping a rock in a lush mountain valley, a cat stalking a pheasant, a shoal of flying fish. Others show elegant ladies in conversation, young people at a drinking party, or a youth somersaulting over the back of a great bull watched by a crowd of courtiers.

The Minoans painted their pictures by a method called fresco. The painter applied his colours directly onto a layer of fresh limeplaster. As the plaster dried, the colours dried and set with it, becoming a permanent part of the wall. The painter had to work quickly, before the plaster dried. If he made a mistake, it could not be rubbed out. He would have to start all over again with a fresh coat of plaster. The speed and confidence with which the Minoan fresco painters worked is reflected in the vigour and dash of the scenes they painted. Here we see Minoan craftsmen decorating a wall in a palace on Crete. On the left, men apply a thick coat of plaster, which they are embossing in relief. On the right a painter applies the pigments to a top coat of plaster.

Their Paints

They used six basic colours, all of them made from rocks and earth native to Crete, ground to a fine powder and mixed with water. Black came from coal. White from slaked lime. Red came from an iron compound called haematite. Yellow came from ochre, a type of earth rich in iron oxides. Blue came from a crystal known as copper silicate. Green was a mixture of the blue and yellow.

In fact, the island of Crete was well-stocked with all the materials that the Minoan builders and painters needed. Timber – a luxury in Egypt and Sumer – was readily available. It was used even in private houses to build a sturdy framework of posts and beams to support walls and upper storeys. Wooden pillars gave further support to horizontal beams. In small houses, the walls were built of unfired mudbrick set on stone foundations and covered with clay plaster. But in grand buildings like the palaces, builders used blocks of Cretan limestone and gypsum – a fine white stone resembling marble or alabaster. Limestone, too, was the source of plaster: the limestone was burnt, then 'slaked' with water to make a crumbly white powder. When mixed with water, the powdery lime made a white plaster which dried to a tough protective coating for outside and inside walls.

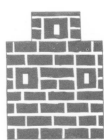

These Minoan painted tiles show that Cretan two-storey houses had windows and shutters, an unknown feature in the Middle East.

29

Grave of the Warrior King

As the Minoans of Crete reached the height of their power in about 2200 BC, groups of tough farmers were becoming established in mainland Greece. These people, sometimes called the Achaeans, built their hilltop towns so as to control the main trade routes. Through trade and raiding the Achaean chieftains amassed rich hoards of gold. From 1600 BC the Achaeans were very influenced in their building by trading contacts with the wealthy and highly developed Minoan civilization. Achaean kings employed Minoan craftsmen to build and decorate their palaces. When, in about 1450 BC, the power of Crete suddenly collapsed, the Achaeans were free to trade, and plunder, all over the Aegean. This period, when warlike Greek kings ruled in palaces such as those in Mycenae, Pylos, Tiryns and Thebes, is called the Mycenaean Age.

Our knowledge of the Minoan and Mycenaean world is only a century old. It comes from the work of an amateur archaeologist, Heinrich Schliemann. Inspired by the literature of Classical Greece (c700–365 BC) he set out to discover the historical reality behind the Greek legends of ancient heroes and battles. The famous Greek epic poem, Homer's *Iliad*, tells how a king of Mycenae, Agamemnon, leads a Greek expedition to besiege and sack the city of Troy. But Homer's world of Bronze Age kings, palaces and warriors was thought to be imaginary. Excavating at Hisarlik (Troy) in Turkey, and at Mycenae and Tiryns in Greece, Schliemann proved beyond doubt that a Greek Bronze Age civilization had flourished 600 years before that of Classical Greece.

One of Schliemann's greatest discoveries was a group of royal graves just inside the ancient citadel at Mycenae. He found the bones of Mycenaean warrior-kings, with their bronze weapons, lying amid incredible treasures of jewels, gold and silver. When he found a golden mask, showing a stern, bearded face, Schliemann was convinced that he was looking at the face of Agamemnon himself!

We now know that these tombs date from a much earlier period than the war against Troy (c1200 BC). But they show the wealth and power of Mycenae at the time that it was coming under Minoan influence. Later, after the fall of Crete, Mycenae became one of the strongest of the Achaean kingdoms of Greece. Homer's famous description of Mycenae 'a strongly founded citadel rich in gold' was no more than the truth.

The kings of Mycenae ruled from a great palace set on the crown of a mountain spur. From here they controlled a surrounding region of fertile farmland stretching to the sea. Below the palace were the large houses of landowning nobles and wealthy merchants and the small dwellings of the common people. The king received a rich income in tribute – labour, agricultural produce and levies on trade – carefully recorded by his palace scribes.

With these resources, kings were able to build on a grand scale. They could import Minoan architects, masons, carpenters and fresco painters to direct the work of Mycenaean craftsmen. Even after the fall of Crete, Mycenaean products were still clearly in the Minoan style.

The beauties of the palace at Mycenae were lost when it was destroyed by fire by invaders during the 12th century BC. Other palaces in Greece suffered the same fate. Only the massively fortified walls, built of huge, irregularly shaped stones, survived. But we do have some complete buildings left to give us an idea of the wealth and power of Mycenaean civilization.

Treasury of Atreus

These are the 'beehive' (tholos) tombs, in which kings were buried in splendour and magnificence. The most famous was discovered by Schliemann himself, who called it 'The Treasury of Atreus' after the mythical father of Agamemnon. It takes the form of a great domed chamber, built entirely of squared and fitted stone blocks on a site cut into the side of a hill. Leading to the chamber is a passage-way – the '*dromos*' – ending at an imposing gateway.

The inner chamber is a corbelled dome – that is, it is constructed from overlapping rings of stone blocks which rise and arch inwards until they meet at the top. The 'steps' where the courses overlapped had then to be *chamfered* – chipped and ground away to make a smooth surface. The inside height of the dome is 13.20 metres, taller than a modern two storey house, and the chamber is 14.50 metres in diameter. It would have been impossible to build a free-standing corbelled dome of this size. Since it was mostly below ground level, however, the builders were able to pack earth around the outside to support it.

On the left, you can see workmen building the dome and the gateway at the end of the dromos. Over 5 metres high, it has just been crowned by an immense inner lintel, a single stone block 8 metres long, 5 metres wide and 1.20 metres thick, weighing some 120 tons.

Far left: A view along the *dromos*, through the ceremonial gateway into the half-completed dome of the Treasury of Atreus. Stoneworkers prepare the stones before they are lifted into place. When the dome is finished, it will be held in place by packing earth around it. It will become part of the hill behind.

Below: Massively fortified walls at the citadel of Mycenae. Later people felt that only giants, like the Cyclops, could have done such work. It is still known as Cyclopean masonry.

Planning a City

The beginning of the 12th century BC was a period of upheaval and disaster for the peoples of the Aegean and Eastern Mediterranean. Mycenaean fortresses were attacked and burned to the ground. Egypt fought off repeated raids by marauding bands known only as 'the Sea Peoples'. Trade and communications collapsed. At the same time, barbarian farmers, armed with iron weapons, moved southwards into central and southern Greece. We cannot be certain of the reasons for these events – but they effectively destroyed civilization in the Aegean. Then, after three centuries new cities started in Greece and the Greek islands. Each city was an independent, self-contained state. They shared a common language, Greek, and a common tradition.

Conditions around the Mediterranean were especially suited to the spread of the Greek way of life. Typical Greek city states (*polis*) were made up of an area of fertile land, and were built so that they were enclosed on three sides by mountains, and open to the sea. This combination is common along every part of the Mediterranean coastline. The climate, too, is predictable: cool, wet winters give way to hot, dry summers. Wherever Greeks settled in the Mediterranean, they could be sure of being able to grow grain, fruit, vegetables, olives and grapes. Finally, the Mediterranean Sea itself encouraged seafaring trade and colonization.

Here is the city-state of Paros, an Aegean island which was famous for its marble quarries. The city itself is built on a spur running out from the mountains behind it. The site is a natural strongpoint. A fortified wall runs up the cliff from the sea and around the back of the city to protect it from attack by sea and land.

At the top of the city is the *acropolis*, 'the high city', with its temples and altars to the gods. It is the place where important religious ceremonies take place – and also where the inhabitants will make a last stand if the city is attacked. Natural springs or wells within the acropolis provide the city with at least part of its water-supply.

Below the acropolis lies a paved open space, the *agora*. The agora is the hub of city life. On market-days farmers sell their produce from stalls set up in the open air. Shady colonnades, *stoa*, run along the sides of the agora: they are meeting places where citizens can talk over their affairs out of the hot sun, or conduct business in the offices and shops of merchants or tradesmen.

Close by the agora is the council chamber, *bouleuterion* – where state affairs are debated and laws passed. There are also offices for the magistrates – the *astynomoi*, who are responsible for streets, water supply and drainage, and the *agoranomoi* who supervise the markets, and trade in general.

The city is divided by wide avenues, *plateiai*, meeting at right angles, and smaller streets and lanes, *stenopoi*. Some parts of the city are reserved for particular trades – the potters' quarter, the metalworkers' quarter and so on. Others are residential areas: private houses are rectangular, built around an open central courtyard.

At the foot of the city is the commercial port, *emporion*. Trading vessels pay taxes for using the port facilities. Some of this money has been spent on building a stone breakwater out into the sea in order to increase the area of sheltered anchorage.

Democracy

The city life of Classical Greece was quite different to that of the Bronze Age Minoans and Mycenaeans. Although Knossos and Mycenae boasted paved streets, private houses and market places, life was dominated by the palace. Kings performed important religious functions which gave them special authority over the whole community. Society was a fixed pyramid, with the king at its head.

A Greek *polis*, on the other hand, was managed by its citizens through political debate and the vote. The city Council, *boule*, could decide to improve the city by building a new

quarter, or extending its harbour. The point was that changes were made in order to benefit the *polis* as a whole, rather than in the interests of a ruling family.

The Greeks themselves wrote a great deal about what city life meant to them. The *polis* was a place where the rights of its citizens were protected by law and where laws were enforced fairly and honestly. It was a centre of trade and industry and the seat of local government. Above all it was a place to which its citizens were proud to belong.

The island city of Paros in the 5th century BC. The stone breakwater extends the already large natural harbour.

Priene, founded in the 4th century BC. The city was cited to take advantage of its dramatic setting and strong natural defences. The acropolis was on the high cliff overlooking the town, which rose in graceful, well-ordered terraces. Within the city were built (1) a temple, (2) a theatre, (3) the town hall, (4) the council, (5) the agora, (6) the gymnasium and (7) the stadium.

Doric

Ionic

Corinthian

The three types, or *orders*, of columns with their carved capitals.

The Parthenon

The early Greeks, like most races, built temples as a house for the gods they worshipped. The task of architecture was to make the house of the gods beautiful which they believed was expressed in perfect proportions. The earliest surviving temples from the 7th century BC already show an awareness of this. Gradually details changed and became more refined. These changes became categorized into orders. The Doric was the earliest and simplest order.

By the 5th century BC, temples had developed from the simple megaron – house of a Mycenaean chief built on a platform in c.1300 BC – to the symmetrical and imposing Temple of Zeus at Olympia of c.470 BC. Temples were now not only places of worship but an illustration of the civic grandeur and power of the city-state concerned.

In 438 BC, the finest example of Doric architecture was finally completed. Its position, perched on the acropolis above the city of Athens, must have been daunting. Here was architecture in the service of politics.

The pride that Greek citizens felt in their polis made them eager to adorn it with fine public buildings – temples, theatres, colonnades. In contrast to this, private houses were very plain. They were made of unfired mudbricks about 40 centimetres square, probably covered with a coat of lime plaster. Even a rich man's house was built in these materials to the same simple design – a one, or two-storey, structure built around an open courtyard. It was as though the Greeks preferred to express their love of fine things in public works rather than through private wealth.

In 447 BC the citizens of Athens began to build a splendid temple to glorify the power and prestige of their polis. It is called the *Parthenon*

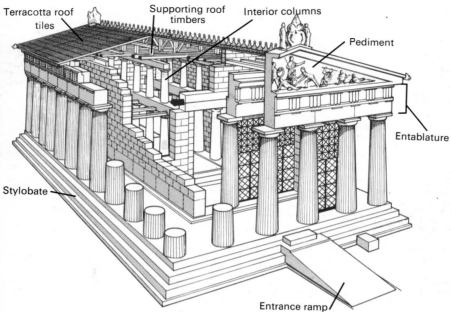

Terracotta roof tiles

Supporting roof timbers

Interior columns

Pediment

Entablature

Stylobate

Entrance ramp

A cutaway view of a Greek Doric temple. The Greeks used post-and-lintel construction – a method which recalled early Greek temples in timber and thatch. Many stone columns were needed to support the heavy beams of stone and timber. Unlike a Christian church, however, a Greek temple was not expected to hold a large number of worshippers. Instead, the Greeks concentrated on designing a well-balanced and proportioned exterior, to be seen from the outside, where ceremonies took place. Hidden iron bars were used to reinforce the stone cross-beams.

A model of the Acropolis, Athens, as it appeared c450 BC. The individual features are numbered as follows:
1. Temple of Athena
2. The Propylaeum (gateway)
3. Statue of Athena
4. The Parthenon
5. Great Altar of Athena
6. Sanctuary of Zeus
7. The Erectheion – a temple housing an ancient image of Athena
8. Administrative offices

and it is the most famous of all Greek buildings. The Athenians were rich with gold looted from the nearby Persian Empire and with funds extorted from their Greek allies. The special goddess of the city, Athena, was thought to have helped Athens in the successful wars against Persia. Now it was time to reward Athena with a new and luxurious temple on Athens' 'high city' – the Acropolis.

Most of the stone for the Parthenon came from the quarries of Mount Pentelicos, about 16 kilometres from Athens. It weighed, altogether, about 22,000 tons. Even today, after many centuries of weathering, the Pentelic marble has an intense brightness in the sunlight. When the stone was newly cut, it was whiter still. Some Athenians thought the Parthenon *too* lavish: they complained that it made Athens look like 'a deceitful woman'. They were probably thinking of its white colour; Athenian women of the time used white make-up, perhaps to hide a sunburnt or wrinkled skin.

The architects of the temple were Ictinos and Callicrates. They designed it to have eight columns across its width and seventeen down its length. These outer columns were of the Doric order, with plain capitals.

Illusions

They have strived for perfection and in doing so have needed to invent new methods to correct faults which the eye rather than the building itself creates. For instance, the columns were cut with a slight taper towards the top – known as *entasis*, which in Greek means 'to strain'. This was to correct the optical illusion by which a straight column seems to narrow in the middle. Furthermore, if all the surfaces of the building were vertical the effect would be to splay the colonnades outwards so scarcely a surface of the building is exactly vertical. The corner columns angle inwards and are thickened to compensate for the illusion, when silhouetted against a light background such as the sky, of fragility or thinness.

Thousands of men were employed in collecting and working the materials for the temple. Sea-captains and their crews brought some of the stone by boat; the roof tiles were made of marble from the island of Paros in the Aegean Sea. Foresters and carpenters prepared cypress wood for the rafters which would support the tiles. Because the temple took about fifteen years to complete, cattle-breeders had time to rear oxen especially for the task of dragging the huge blocks of Pentelic marble up the Acropolis. For decoration, sculptors cut fluting down every column. The near perfect roundness of the capitals of the columns may have been produced by turning the stones on a lathe.

To make the stones of the temple fit tightly together, the faces of the adjacent blocks were rubbed together. The friction wore away any lumps, allowing the two surfaces to lie flush.

It is not often realised that large quantities of metal were used in building the Parthenon. Metal clamps were sunk into the blocks where they joined, keeping them tightly linked together. And where there was an unusually heavy load to carry, beams of iron were hidden in the stone to strengthen it.

There were many stone statues and reliefs on the building, as we shall see. They were designed by the sculptor Pheidias, and bronze was used to decorate some of them. Figures of horses were fitted with bronze bridles. This metal has long ago been plundered, but in the horses' heads and necks we can still see the drill-holes which were made to hold the bridles in place. Meanwhile other temples and a gateway – *propylaeum* – were being built on the acropolis. Most, like the exquisite Temple of Athena Paros or *Erectheion* were to honour the goddess Athena, others were to honour gods such as Zeus.

When it was finally completed, in 438 BC, the Parthenon was one of the greatest masterpieces of the ancient world. Its brilliant white columns and vividly coloured statues and reliefs shone out across the city – a fitting monument to the Golden Age of Greece.

In a Greek marble quarry, quarrymen drive wooden wedges into cracks in the rock – splitting it off into regular blocks. Other workers move blocks in a collapsible iron cage fitted with wheels.

Quarrying

The Greeks were lucky enough to have excellent sources of fine quality marble for their public buildings. The most famous quarries were those at Mount Pentelicos, and on the island of Paros. Marble naturally tends to split into parallel blocks. The Greeks quarried it by driving wedges into faults in the rock and splitting it away from its bed. They cut it into regular blocks with a smooth-bladed bronze saw. As the saw was drawn back and forth, the blade was fed with a mixture of water and sand. In this way it was possible to cut through the marble without splintering it. The Greek quarrymen transported the marble blocks from the quarry in a number of ways. One method was to leave a projecting keyhole shaped piece on top of the block when it was being sawn into shape. This piece had a hole bored through it, so that the quarrymen could thread a rope through it and haul the block away with a rope and pulley. Another method was to fit the block with iron wedges, called 'lewises', which had a ring on the outside. Using a simple type of crane, the Greeks fixed metal callipers onto the lewis pieces: even very heavy blocks could be lifted in this way. Above, you can see workers moving a large block in a kind of wheeled cage, thus converting an awkward rectangular object into one which could easily be moved by rolling. When it was necessary to move heavy blocks over long distances, the blocks were loaded onto ox-carts; sometimes thirty or forty oxen were needed to drag a single huge block.

The Megaron

The Greeks particularly liked to use marble for their temples. The shape of a Greek temple was very ancient. It was based on the *megaron* – a type of house dating from Mycenaean times. The *megaron* had a porch, leading into a small anteroom, which in turn led into a large room. Some of the earliest temples had walls made entirely of mud, with roofs of timber and thatch. But by about 800 BC wooden posts were being used in rows – one post under the centre of each roof beam, as a support, and other posts set into the mud walls to support the ends of the beam. Some of the early temples were built on a platform of stone. If set in earth, the posts might slowly have sunk under the weight of the roof, twisting the building out of shape.

By the 500s BC, stone columns were taking the place of wooden posts, as the Greek communities grew wealthier. The early stone columns were very plain. In later temples however, the columns were decorated with ornamental capitals – the sections at the heads of the columns. The different types of columns were given particular names – the Doric order, the Ionic order and the Corinthian order (see previous page).

A column of a Greek temple was not made from one huge piece of stone. It was usually formed from many stones, sometimes called 'drums', which were circular in cross-section, and rested one on another. They were not fixed together with cement, but each drum had, at bottom and top, a hole for a thick wooden peg. This peg also fitted into the next drum, and so prevented the drums from getting out of alignment. On the right, in the scaffolding, workmen are building the columns, by putting the 'drums' of stone on top of each other. Knobs of stone were left for a time on the outside of the drum. Ropes were tied to these knobs, so that the drums could be hoisted into place. Some of the rectangular stones have 'U'-shaped cuts, to hold the ropes which will hoist them into position across the tops of the columns.

Although the Greek temples seem very large, there was very little room inside them. The heart of the temple was the *cella*, where a statue of the god stood. But the Greeks did not go inside the temple to worship. They sacrificed to the god at an altar outside the temple porch. They took their offering into the temple and then came to worship at an altar outside the temple porch where they sacrificed an animal, such as an ox, to the gods.

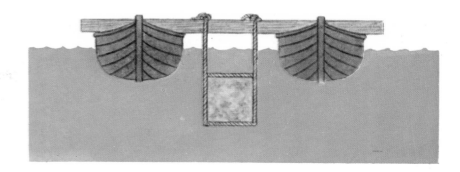

Above: Transporting a large stone block by sea. It has been suspended from a beam across two boats. Because it is fully immersed, the block has lost weight through displacement.

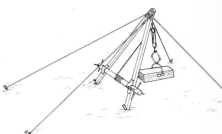

Right: A diagram of the windlass hoist being used in the scene below. The tongs are attached to metal wedges in the stone block.

Below: A Greek architect directs the construction of a Doric temple. The heavy stone blocks have been brought from a nearby quarry by ox-wagon. They have special channels cut into them to take ropes which are used to drag them into position. In the background, columns are built up from circular stone drums: these have projecting bosses by which they can be hoisted up by the men operating the windlass.

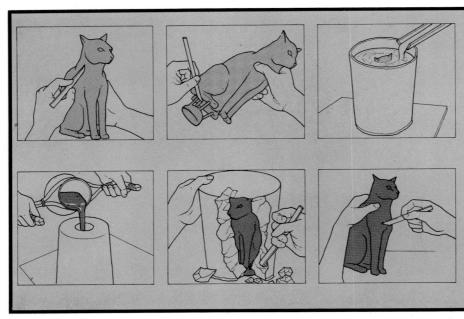

After 2000 BC, Egyptian metalworkers made great advances in casting methods. As a result, they were able to produce better tools in copper and bronze, and also larger objects and figures. An important technique was the 'lost wax' process. First, the object was carefully modelled in soft wax, shaped around a hard clay core. Next, the model was coated with fine clay, which was allowed to dry hard. A funnel was left in the base of the mould. The mould was then baked, melting the wax which ran out through the funnel. Then the molten metal was poured into the funnel, replacing the molten wax. When the bronze had cooled, the outer mould was broken open to reveal the bronze casting. Further finishing and polishing was necessary before the object was finally completed.

Craftsmen in Bronze

This *caryatid* is part of the colonnade that supports the roof of the porch of the Erectheion on the Acropolis at Athens. The sculptor has skilfully carved the girl's hairstyle so as to strengthen the neck of the statue without making it look unnaturally thick. Caryatid means 'female figure used as a pillar'.

The Greeks produced some of the finest statuary of the ancient world. By the 5th century BC, Greek sculptors had become masters at creating lifelike images in marble and bronze. The images were based on observation of the real world. But, unlike the Romans, the Greeks were not interested in making purely realistic sculpture. Rather they tried to portray ideal qualities such as strength, courage and nobility. So, often, Greek statues show a perfection that cannot be found in the real world.

It became usual for the Greeks to decorate their temples with sculptures. The pediments – the shallow triangles at each end of the temple, above the colonnade – were natural frames for statuary. On the Parthenon, they contained free-standing statues of Athena the virgin (in Greek *parthenos*, hence the name of the temple), and Poseidon with other gods. Below them was the frieze, a band of carved stonework set at roof level, which ran along all four sides of the temple. The frieze is divided into *triglyphs* – elements in relief shaped like a Roman III, which alternate with *metopes* – carvings of figures standing out from the flat stonework. They depict the fight between humans and Centaurs. Centaurs are mythical beasts – half human, half horse – who fought the Lapiths – a tribe who lived in Northern Greece. The battle started because the drunken Centaurs disgraced themselves at the marriage of Hippodamia to the Lapith king, Pirithous. Another frieze skirts the *cella* or inner temple. This depicts the Panathenaic procession of youths and maidens bringing the sacred cloak – *peplos* – to the goddess, Athena.

All the statues and carvings on the Parthenon were designed by Pheidias – one of the greatest sculptors ever to have lived. They depicted the triumphs of Athena and battle scenes from Greek mythology. Armed warriors and plunging horses are so powerfully sculpted that, even in the fragments that remain, they seem about to spring into life.

These statues were made of Pentelic marble, like almost all the rest of the Parthenon. They were sculpted, piece by piece, in Pheidias's workshop by assistants under his direction, before being transported to the Parthenon and hoisted into position. Nowadays, the surviving fragments have a plain creamy colour. But when they were new they were brightly painted. Small traces of paint are still sometimes found, but no Greek statue has survived with its full colouring. Even in ancient times, the colours faded and occasionally needed renewing. Melted wax was worked into the surfaces with a

hot iron, to insulate against rain and protect the colours.

A Greek sculptor used a wooden mallet and a set of chisels to create a statue from a block of stone. The final smoothness was obtained by rubbing the stone with an abrasive substance, such as pumice.

Drills were also used, in the shape of a brace and bit, or driven by a bow with the bowstring looped round the drill. The second type of drill could make the deep channels which represented the folds of clothing.

Bronze Statues

Greek sculptors also cast their statues in bronze. A lost masterpiece of Pheidias was the superb bronze and ivory statue of the goddess Athena, some 13 metres high, which once stood inside the Parthenon. It was clothed in a robe of pure gold, made up of detachable plates. In wartime, the gold could be taken off and melted down to make coins, to pay Athens' soldiers and sailors. In peacetime, when the state treasury had recovered, new gold plates could be attached to the robe. The story goes that Pheidias designed the robe in this way so that his fellow Athenians could take off the gold and weigh it, to check that he had not stolen any!

Here you can see a Greek foundry where bronze statues are being cast and assembled. The founder pours the molten bronze into prepared moulds (see Lost Wax Process above). One worker breaks open the clay mould to show the cast head of a goddess. Another cleans off the rough bits from the surface of a cast section. On the right skilled finishers work on a bronze figure of a god, assembled from a number of separately cast pieces. They are burnishing and polishing the statue to remove all traces of the joins between the separately cast pieces.

A Greek bronze foundry, mid 5th century BC. The man in the foreground breaks open the mould of the head of a goddess. The spikey bits are the 'leads' out of which the melted wax has run. (See Lost Wax Process above).

Temple of Solomon

In about 1200 BC, the 12 Hebrew tribes, under the leadership of Joshua, re-entered the land of Palestine. They conquered the neighbouring tribes, and for two hundred years they fought against the Philistines from the coast, until David (1004–965 BC) conquered them and established the kingdom of Israel. He also defeated the Jebusites and made their city, Jerusalem, his capital. His son, Solomon, (961–922 BC) organized what was by now a small empire. He divided it into 12 districts and imposed heavy taxes to pay for an ambitious building programme. These taxes, together with profits from trade with Egypt and Asia Minor, enabled Solomon to enlarge cities and found new ones. The cities were garrisons for his army – a powerful force of cavalry and chariots. One of Solomon's greatest works was the contruction of the Temple at Jerusalem, which housed the Ark of the Covenant, the sacred relic of the Jewish people.

'Then Solomon began to build the house of the Lord at Jerusalem in mount Moriah, where the Lord appeared unto David his father . . . In the fourth year of Solomon's reign over Israel . . . he began to build the house of the Lord.'

II Chronicles 3, 1; I Kings 6, 1

The works of David and Solomon are examples of how strong the building tradition was in the Near East. To build his temple, Solomon turned to his ally and trading partner, the Phoenician, King Hiram of Tyre. The Phoenicians of Lebanon were traders and seafarers, famous for the skill of their craftsmen. They controlled the dense juniper and cedar forests of Lebanon, which supplied the finest building timber for the valley civilizations of Egypt and Mesopotamia.

Materials
The architect of Solomon's temple was a Phoenician from Tyre. Many of the craftsmen – masons, carpenters, goldsmiths, bronzesmiths – working on it were also Phoenicians. Solomon also conscripted thousands of workers from Israel to provide unskilled labour. Materials were ordered: cedarwood from Lebanon, gold from the mines of Parvaim in Arabia, copper from southern Palestine, building stone from local quarries.

The temple was to stand on a stone platform about 3 metres high. The stone blocks arrived ready cut and dressed from the stonemasons' workshops. Here you can see the building operations in progress. The basic structure of the temple is a framework of massive cedarwood posts and beams. The interior is to be the *Hekal*, or Holy Place. The doorway leads in to a small, windowless room, the *Debir*, or Holy of Holies, which will hold the Ark.

The inside walls of these chambers will later be panelled with gilded cedarwood. Meanwhile, a worker puts the finishing touches to one of the two bronze pillars which will eventually stand on either side of the doorway. According to the Bible, the pillars had bronze capitals decorated with cast pomegranates and lilies, and were some 15 metres high. The doors of the temple, too, were cast in bronze.

To the left of the temple stands an enormous bronze bowl, supported on the shoulders of 12 bronze oxen. The Bible calls it a 'Sea', for it was said to hold 45,460 litres (10,000 gallons) of water. This masterpiece of the bronzeworker's

art was to suffer a sad fate. In 734 BC, King Ahaz of Jerusalem was forced to send the oxen as tribute to the Assyrian king. The bowl itself was broken up and carried off to Babylon in 587 BC after Jerusalem was captured by Nebuchadnezzar.

The building of the temple took seven years. When completed it was 28 metres long by 9 metres wide by 15 metres high. A three-storied gallery surrounded the temple on three sides. It held treasure chambers and rooms for the temple priests. The ceremonial furnishings of the temple were magnificent: a golden altar for sacrifices, together with lampstands, knives, incense vessels, and tables for offerings – all of pure gold or goldplated bronze.

When the day came for the Ark to be brought to the temple, countless sheep and oxen were sacrificed. Priests carried the Ark, containing the two stone tablets of the Covenant, from Zion, David's fortress. They passed into the temple through the great bronze doors, decorated with palm trees, flowers and winged figures – cherubim and seraphim. The Ark was placed in the Holy of Holies. Two large, bronze cherubim, with spread wings, were placed on the Ark to guard it.

Solomon intended his temple to stand forever, but it was not to be. Some more of its treasures had to be given up as tribute to the Assyrians. Then in 597 BC, Nebuchadnezzar of Babylon captured Jerusalem: '*And he carried out thence all the treasures of the house of the Lord and the treasures of the king's house . . . And he carried away all Jerusalem, and all the princes, and all the mighty men of valour, even ten thousand captives . . . save the poorest sort of the people of the land.*' II Kings 24. Then, in 586 BC, Babylonian armies overran Jerusalem for a second time. City and temple were completely destroyed, and the remaining population taken off as captives to Babylon. There they remained until 538 BC, when King Cyrus of Persia allowed them to return to Palestine. They quickly started to restore the temple.

Left: 'And the king commanded, and they brought great stones, costly stones and hewed stones, to lay the foundation of the house. And Solomon's builders and Hiram's builders did hew them, and the stone-squarers; so they prepared timber and stones to build the house'.
(*I Kings 5: 17–18*)

Right: The flat-roofed houses of Jerusalem had protective parapets around their roofs. A houseowner could be sued under Jewish law if his guest fell over the edge!

Assyria, Land of Palaces

The land of Assyria lay in the upper valley of the River Tigris. It commanded important land routes running both North–South and East–West. Asshur, its chief city, was a trading centre from at least 1900 BC. Although not always an autonomous state (it maintained its identity until after about 1350 BC) warlike Assyrian rulers imposed their rule over a wide area. In the 9th century BC, after a period of fluctuating fortunes the so-called neo-Assyrian empire began. The centre of power moved 100 km north from Asshur to Kalhu and Nineveh.

Assyrian power depended on well-equipped and ruthless armies of charioteers and archers. Assyrian kings led devastating raids against their neighbours, massacring huge numbers of people and carrying off loot. Between 745 BC and 660 BC, the Assyrians ruled the empire stretching from Elam in Khuzistan to Syria and Palestine and, eventually, to Egypt.

Although they were merciless conquerors, the Assyrian kings were also great builders. Nearly every ruler built himself a new palace, or remodelled an existing one. Tukulti-Ninurta I (1244–1208 BC) built himself a new capital north of Assur. Assur-nasir-apli II (883–859 BC) ordered the building of a magnificent new palace at Kalhu (Nimrud) on the Tigris. It was of mudbrick, decorated with multi-coloured patterns of glazed brick, and covered with limestone slabs carved with scenes of battles and hunting. The palace gardens, filled with plants from every part of the Assyrian empire, were watered by a canal specially dug from the nearby river Zab. The king himself wrote of the beauty of his palace, and recorded that 69,574 guests were invited to its opening celebrations. The king's son Shalmaneser III built another palace at Kalhu: this had three great courtyards for parading troops. In all, it measured 350 metres by 250 metres, with walls 4.5 metres thick and perhaps 12 metres in height.

Fort Sargon

Sargon II (722–705 BC), not content with restoring the original palace at Kalhu, planned to build an entirely new capital to be called Dur-Sharruken ('Fort Sargon'). Treasures were brought from far and wide to decorate the royal palace, which was to be the centrepiece of a vast new city. Whole populations (including Israelites) were transported from the provinces to turn Sargon's plans into reality. They worked alongside armies of prisoners, together with communities of skilled craftsmen imported from Syria and Phoenicia (Lebanon).

Building began in 717 BC. Huge cedar trunks were brought 800 kilometres from the Mediterranean coast to make the roof-beams, door-posts and doors of the palace. It was built on an immense platform, 14 metres in height, which was to carry the palace, temples, and residences for the royal household. The whole complex was enclosed by a fortified wall nearly 9 kilometres long, with eight gateways.

As usual, unfired mudbrick was used for all the main structures. But the Assyrians also had good sources of stone for facing and decoration. The palace platform was given an outer casing of fitted limestone blocks, each of which measure $2 \times 2 \times 2.75$ metres and weighed about 23 tons. The palace walls were covered with sculptured gypsum slabs standing as high as 2.5 or 3 metres, showing scenes of Sargon's exploits and power. The palace gates were guarded by massive figures of winged bulls with human heads. These were carved out of single blocks of gypsum about $4.4 \times 4.4 \times 0.60$ metres, weighing some 20 tons. The figures were roughly chipped out by masons at the quarries, then transported to the site, where the detailed finishing and polishing was carried out.

After ten years, the palace was completed and Sargon was able to dedicate his new capital to the gods. A festival was held, attended by the Assyrian nobles, state officials, provincial governers and the rulers of states which were under

Assyrian rule. Strangely, however, Sargon's grandiose dream proved a failure. The great city he planned remained unfinished, and was abandoned soon after his death in 705 BC – a deserted monument to the might of Assyria.

Transport of Materials

The reconstruction on this page is based on Assyrian stone reliefs which show very clearly how such palaces were built. Wherever possible, materials were transported by water. In the foreground, a circular leather coracle is used to carry the bronze sockets in which the palace doorposts will fit. To the right a heavy stone block is being floated down river on a raft made from logs tied to inflated animal hides. On the river bank, an Assyrian king watches prisoners drag a half-finished stone statue from the quarry to the new palace. It is being transported on a giant wooden sled hauled over rollers. As the party in front pull on heavy cables, probably made from reeds, another group helps to ease the sled along with a stout wooden lever. The statue will be set up, with another, to guard the palace gateway from enemies and evil spirits. When carved and polished, it will be the shape of a human-headed, winged bull. Elsewhere, two men are pulling a wheeled wagon carrying cedar and fir timber from the Mediterranean coast. Ahead of them, one man carries iron axes for cutting the timber, while another carries a large two-handed metal saw.

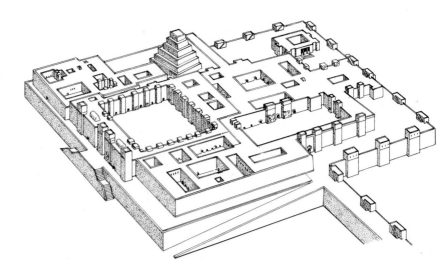

Sargon II's palace at his new capital Khorsabad (Dur-Sharruken) was built in about 710 BC. It was contained within a walled area of some 2.6 square kilometres. The main structure was mudbrick, faced with wall reliefs in carved stone and decorated with huge human-headed winged bulls. Besides the domestic quarters, the palace included administrative halls, temples and a beautifully carved pyramid ziggurat. The ziggurat was built to honour an Assyrian god whose shrine was on the top.

An Assyrian king surveys the transport of materials to the site of his new palace. His trumpeters help to make a celebration of the occasion. All the details in this reconstruction are based on Assyrian stone carvings.

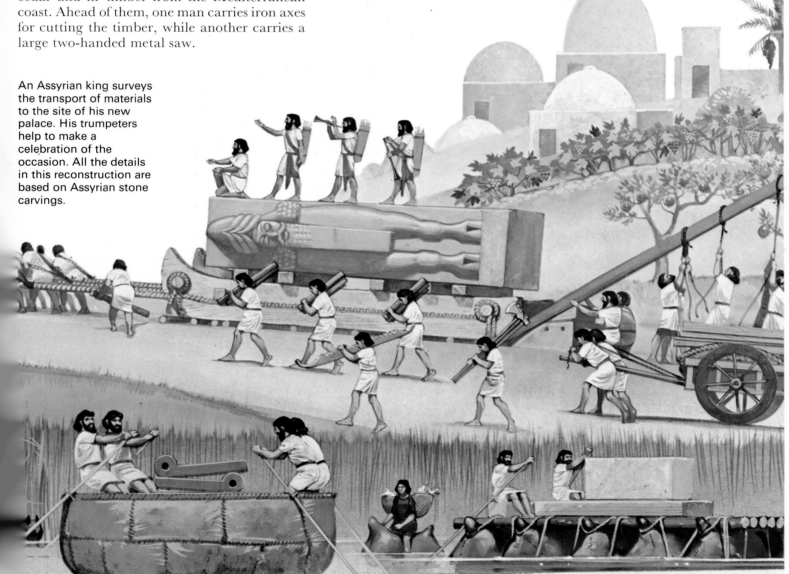

The Great Wall

In China a civilization developed which owed very little to the outside world. Farming was carried on in the fertile valley of the Hwang Ho, or Yellow River, from about 5000 BC. The first strong, centralized kingdom was established by the rulers of the Shang Dynasty (1500–1027 BC). Bronze weapons were made and the horse-drawn chariot was introduced, together with a form of writing. Under the later Chou Dynasty (1027–221 BC) China broke up into a number of rival states, perpetually at war. Finally the state of Ch'in emerged victorious. Its ruler, Prince Cheng, brutally imposed a single system of government over all China. In 221 BC, he proclaimed himself Shih Huang-ti, the 'First Emperor'. The empire he founded lasted in various forms until 1912 AD.

In Chinese history, Shih Huang-ti was credited with the construction of China's greatest monument, the Great Wall. In fact, the First Emperor's achievement was to link up existing sections of the defensive walls built by the feudal states originally to protect their territory from rapacious neighbours in the anarchic Chou period. The purpose of the new wall was to defend the mountainous northern border of China against attacks by nomadic horsemen –

the Huns – from the Gobi Desert of central Asia. When completed, the Great Wall ran continuously for about 2250 kilometres, studded with watchtowers and massive forts. It was built by the forced labour of armies of peasants, thousands of whom perished in the harsh northern winters.

Rammed Earth

The Wall is built from rammed earth, a traditional method of Chinese construction. Soil was pounded between shuttering made from wooden planks. Then the shuttering was removed, and another layer of rammed earth added in the same way, using the first as a foundation. Bamboo was placed between the layers, to help them dry out. When the wall was completed, its sides were faced with burnt brick or plaster.

At its highest the Great Wall rises to 12 metres – a formidable barrier against the mounted raiders it was intended to keep out. Along the top of the wall runs a roadway about 8 metres wide – sufficient for a detachment of the emperor's cavalry to move quickly to deal with any trouble reported along the wall. Watchtowers, like the one on the left might only be manned by a few men. But in an emergency they lit signal fires to summon troops from one of the great forts which guarded the main passes into China.

Chinese Houses

Wall-building is one of the most ancient of Chinese skills. Every Chinese city was su

rounded by a stout defensive wall. Even within the city walls, further walls divided one part of the city from another, and traffic had to pass through a series of gateways, manned by officials. In northern China, the villages were very much at risk from nomad attack, so they too were surrounded by mud walls. Here the peasants lived in simple thatched huts with thick walls of rammed earth. In the towns, the wealthy merchants and nobility lived in elegant timber-framed houses within walled courtyards. The wooden pillars and beams which form the main structure of the house were gaily painted and lacquered. Lacquer is the sap of an oak tree which when heated becomes soft and black. When hard it can be polished until its surface becomes like glass. Pigments can be added.

Houses often had more than one courtyard. Built into the wall of the outer courtyard would have been a watchtower from which guards at night kept a constant lookout for intruders. In the second courtyard there were a number of buildings. One would hold the bedrooms and private sitting rooms, a large one for the master and a smaller one for his wife. Another building would be the banqueting hall with richly decorated cushions, silk wall-hangings and rugs. We know the type of houses people lived in from models found in tombs of the period.

In central China, timber was rather scarce, so Chinese builders developed a special way of using it. The foundation of the house was a platform of rammed earth. Timber posts, widely spaced, were set into the corners of the foundations to

make a rectangle. The post heads were fitted into a series of special wooden brackets, *tou-kung*, which looked something like a branched candlestick. The brackets helped spread the load of the horizontal roof timbers, and kept the number of vertical posts to the minimum. The walls of timber-framed houses were lightly built of plaster, matting or lattice. The houses were crowned with tent-like roofs of shiny coloured tiles, made of glazed pottery. The roof ends are finished off with round tiles decorated with fabulous beasts.

Above: The Great Wall of China. On the right hand side, peasant labourers excavate the earth and ram it into place using wooden frames. To the left, a completed section of wall, with its battlements and metalled roadway, leads to a fortified watchtower.

Left: Pottery model of a house from the Chinese Han period (25–220 AD). The spreading brackets, *tou-kung*, which support the rafters can be clearly seen under the eaves of the roofs. The house has a double gateway, leading into a courtyard – a classic pattern for Chinese houses.

The Achievement of Rome

Some stages in the construction of a Roman aqueduct. At bottom right, surveyors map out the line with a groma. Carpenters assemble wooden centering for the arches. Note that stone is used only for the outer casing of the structure – the inner core is of concrete.

By 250 BC the city of Rome was the strongest power in the Italian peninsula. In two hundred years the Romans went on to take control of the turbulent states and kingdoms surrounding the Mediterranean. Eventually, Roman rule extended from Britain to Mesopotamia, the largest empire the world had ever seen. Throughout their vast empire the Romans imposed orderly government, encouraged trade, improved existing towns and cities and founded new ones.

In Mediterranean Europe, city life first developed under the Greeks. The Romans carried on the tradition in their own colonization of Celtic Europe. The Roman city was the natural unit of local government in the provinces. It was a centre where troops could be garrisoned and from which Roman law could be enforced. It was also the marketplace for local farm produce and local industry, as well as a focus for general trade. With its well-planned streets and houses and its public facilities such as the city baths, water supply and drainage, the Roman city provided its inhabitants with a comfortable and secure way of life.

The Romans were extremely practical builders and planners. All their projects were undertaken with a view to improving the trade and wealth of the empire. They built paved roads, bridged rivers and founded thriving new towns and cities. One of the greatest Roman achievements was to provide their cities with a permanent supply of running water.

The Aqueduct

A Roman city received its water from one or more aqueducts. Stone conduits brought water

from the nearest available natural source. Sometimes the sources were miles away. Of the four aqueducts serving Lugdunum (Lyon) in Roman Gaul, one was 74.8 kilometres long, another 60.8 kilometres. Engineering feats like these freed Roman cities from the need to be close to a single water source. They could be built at sites which were best for exploiting trade, which meant that cities could support larger populations than ever before.

In a Roman aqueduct the water ran downhill from a high source – perhaps a mountain lake – to the centre of population that it served. At the downhill end, the water discharged into a great artificial reservoir. From here the water travelled through clay or hollowed out timber, or lead pipes to public fountains, lavatories and baths, and to the private houses of rich citizens (who paid a rent for the privilege). In AD 97, the nine aqueducts of Rome provided 32 million gallons of water per day, enough to serve the whole of Rome for cleaning, feeding and power.

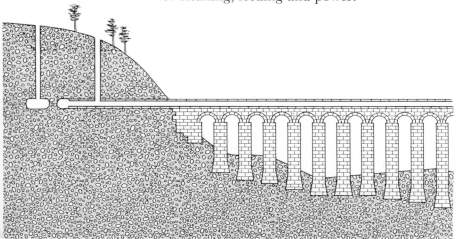

Driving an aqueduct through a hill. Workers sank a series of shafts into the ground. At the bottom a tunnel was dug in both directions. The piers are built at different heights so as to obtain a level gradient above uneven ground. The tunnel had to have just the right degree of slope.

It was very important to get the gradient, or slope, of the aqueduct just right, so that the water would flow at a steady pace. Surveyors calculated the line that the aqueduct had to follow. Where the ground rose above the line, the aqueduct would have to run through an underground tunnel. In places where the ground level was below the line of the aqueduct, it would have to be carried on supporting arches built on massive square piers. The burden of paying for the aqueducts fell mostly on the imperial treasury in Rome. Where possible, they were paid for either by profits from the spoils of war or by wealthy public benefactors.

Pipelines

Clearly building tunnels or piers takes a great deal of time, manpower and money. So in some cases, the Romans adopted a cheaper and quicker alternative. At Asperidos in Turkey, and as part of the water system at Lincoln, the Romans built pipelines. This creates a siphon effect and allows water to 'flow' uphill. One of the drawbacks to this system is that if the pressure suddenly increases, the pipe cracks. So, the Romans built 'header' tanks. These were sections where the pipeline went sharply uphill and then downhill, so that when water rushed into them, its momentum was reduced.

A Roman aqueduct is being built out from the hillside across a plain. It looks something like a railway viaduct. At first sight it seems to be built of solid stone, but if you look at the half-completed pier on the right, you can see that the stone is only an outer skin, or facing. The hollow interior will be filled with Roman concrete – a mixture of lime, volcanic ash, gravel and water which dries into a solid rock-like mass.

To the left you can see a group of men using a wooden hoist to raise the outer stones of an arch, which is being built around a semi-circular wooden form – the *centering*. When the stone outer casing is complete, the hollow space within will also be filled with concrete. After the concrete has dried, the wooden centering will be taken down.

The water itself will run through a rectangular stone channel, which is loosely covered to keep out the dirt. Part of this has already been built out from the hill. The channel is lined with a special, water-resistant type of concrete.

Concrete

The Romans pioneered the use of concrete to build arches. Because they were lighter, concrete arches could be supported on slimmer piers than arches made of solid brick or stone. Also, since most of the structure was solid concrete, the skilled work of cutting and fitting stone, or laying bricks, was kept to a minimum. With these methods, using auxiliary workers culled from the Roman army the Romans were able to build an aqueduct at the rate of about 8 kilometres a year. The fact that many sections of Roman aqueducts are still standing shows just how reliable their methods were.

In a Roman Town

Before the Romans conquered Celtic Europe, fine houses of brick or stone with tiled roofs were unknown. Traditional materials – wood, thatch and daub – were used, although the floor area of round 'huts', excavated in Britain may be equivalent in size to a modern four bedroomed house.

Perhaps because of increasing trade and contact with the Greeks and then the Romans, towns did develop in Celtic areas, but they were a poor reflection of the fine cities of the Romans. Celtic towns did not boast paved streets or piped water. But the switch to life based on the city followed rapidly after the conquest by the Romans.

The Romans founded towns which were well-planned and solidly built in brick and stone. The neat, comfortable houses being built here could have been built in almost any town in Roman Europe. You can also see some of the materials and skills that made the Romans such effective builders.

House Building

Moulded bricks of baked clay were an all-purpose Roman building material. They have been used to build the pillars of the house in the foreground, and also the walls of the half completed building across the street. Moulded clay roof tiles replace traditional European thatch. Here you can see the two complementary kinds: the flat type with upturned edges which forms the main surface of the roof, and the semi-circular tiles which cover the joints between them. The plaster being used on the wall and the pillar is another important material It is a mixture of lime, sand and water: in different strengths the mixture could make a mortar for jointing bricks, or a strong concrete for large-scale building. In the background you can see a wooden crane with which the Romans were able to lift heavy weights. It is powered by two men who turn the big wheel by walking inside it – as it turns, the lifting rope is wound round a drum. In the foreground, a man uses a simple rope and pulley to lift a basket of plaster.

The whole scene, right down to the efficient, modern looking tools the men are using, gives an impression of purposefulness and ordered effort. Indeed, the Roman towns and cities of Europe were built to high standards, unsurpassed until the 18th and 19th centuries.

Roman craftsmen and labourers at work building a town in a newly settled European province. Roman town and city planning brought a high standard of comfort to citizens of the empire.

Roman tools show striking similarities to those used by craftsmen today.

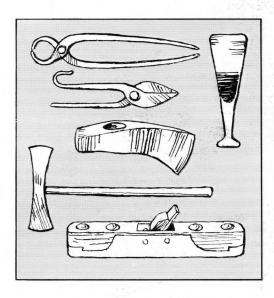

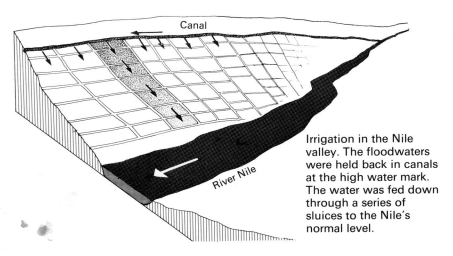

Irrigation in the Nile valley. The floodwaters were held back in canals at the high water mark. The water was fed down through a series of sluices to the Nile's normal level.

Building Canals

The first civilizations started in valleys where the soil was rich, but where the summers were hot and dry. This was true of Egypt, Mesopotamia, the Indus valley of ancient India, and the Yellow River valley of China. To take advantage of highly fertile land, it was necessary to water the crops in the dry season, and then to protect the fields against uncontrolled flooding. All the valley civilizations developed large-scale systems of flood control and artificial irrigation. The need to keep these systems in repair led to efficient governments, which organized the work of digging and clearing canals and ditches to water the fields. Once this had been done, the land could produce enough food, year after year, to support very large populations.

Irrigation

According to Babylonian myth, *Kur*, the flood-dragon, was conquered by *Ninurta*, who created the world by holding back the floodwaters behind a great dam. This ancient story describes very well how the peoples of Mesopotamia managed to grow their crops. In the south (ancient Sumer) the land is very flat. The Tigris and Euphrates flood in April–June, when crops are already growing in the fields. Dams of mudbrick had to be built to contain the floods. The water was then led down to the fields during the hot months by a series of canals and ditches. The beds and banks of these waterways were made from mudbrick, lined with reed matting and a coating of bitumen – a sticky, black tar which occurred naturally in the region. Enormous work was involved in the construction of these canals. The Nahrwan canal, for example, was at least 100 kilometres long and 12 metres wide. Just as important was the work of maintaining them. If they were allowed to silt up, the waterflow would stop. But if the water flowed too fast, the current would undermine the banks and wash them away. The great king Hammurabi of Babylon devoted part of his famous code of laws to the problem. Every man, he said, must keep his own part of the ditch system in repair. If he failed to do so, he had to repay his neighbour for any damage caused. Each district was made responsible for the upkeep of the canals which flowed through it. The concern with the life-giving water system was part of everybody's life. Even in school, children were given mathematical problems which asked them to calculate how long it would take a certain number of men to dig a fixed length of canal.

Bavian-Nineveh Canal

From very early times, then, rulers in Mesopotamia saw it as part of their duty to extend and improve the irrigation systems. The Assyrian king Sennacherib (705–681 BC) built a great freshwater canal in 691 BC. It brought water from Bavian, in the foothills of the north, to the city of Nineveh, a distance of 80 kilometres. The canal was made of stone, quarried from very close to where it began at Bavian. More than two million blocks were used. Each block measured about $50 \times 50 \times 65$ centimetres.

The lining of the canal was made up of bitumen, concrete and a layer of limestone paving. While it was still being built, the bed of the canal was used as a roadway along which the stone from the Bavian quarries was transported on wheels or rollers. Along its course, mountain streams were dammed behind stone weirs. Adjustable gates, called sluices, were built into the dam walls. They could be raised or lowered to control the amount of water fed into the completed canal.

Canal building and maintenance was a traditional duty of Mesopotamian rulers. The astounding fertility of the region depended on it. The Assyrian king Sennacherib (705–681 BC) built a complex system of canals to provide Nineveh, his capital, with drinking water and water for the fields. Beyond the canal, the cliff face has been carved with gigantic figures of gods, together with that of the king himself. An inscription in the rock proudly records that Sennacherib saw his great canal finished in only 15 months.

Roads

Until 1000 BC there were no roads other than ancient footpaths and trackways. The light, horsedrawn chariot could be driven on any open country and did not need them. Ox-drawn carts were too clumsy to cover any but very short distances. It was not until people bred a type of horse able to carry a rider for long distances that regular overland travel at any speed became a possibility. Even then water transport remained the cheapest method of moving heavy cargoes.

Assyrian Roads

The first people to build roads were the Assyrians. One Assyrian king recorded how his engineers 'hewed a way with bronze pickaxes and made passable a passage for my chariot and my troops'. A 'road' like this was no more than a roughly levelled, unpaved track, with guard houses set along it at intervals.

The Assyrian type of well-policed military road was taken up and improved by the Persians. By 500 BC, the Persian Empire stretched from Anatolia (Turkey) to Afghanistan. Persian kings ruled through a highly organized system of local officials, who were directed by royal commands. Their orders were carried on horseback by royal messengers, riding along well-maintained roads. The roads, levelled and partly paved, were policed by guards stationed at rest-houses every 24 kilometres. The mes-

Chinese roadbuilding rivalled that of Rome. Wooden bridges carried them over rivers, and wooden trestles supported roads cut into steep mountainsides.

A working party of Roman soldiers on roadbuilding duties. The road surface is curved (cambered) so that water will run off into the ditches. The layers of gravel, rubble, concrete and paving made Roman roads exceptionally rugged. The Romans intended roads for military use rather than as routes for trade and travel. Milestones, the height of a man, were placed every 1000 Roman paces – *passuum*. Engraved on them was the distance in *mille passum* from Rome.

sengers could obtain fresh horses at these way-stations. A famous Persian road ran from Susa, in Persia, via Babylon, to Sardis on the Aegean coast of Anatolia – a distance of 2560 kilometres. Messages passed from Susa to Babylon at an average speed of 160 kilometres a day.

Roman Roads

Apart from the Chinese (see illustration above), no people built true road systems until the Romans. The first Roman road, the Appian Way, was begun in 312 BC. Eventually it linked Rome with the south of Italy. By 200 AD, the Roman road system stretched from Hadrian's Wall in Scotland to the Euphrates.

Roman roads were designed first and fore-most to move troops quickly and to send orders from Rome to distant provinces. There were three main classes of road: paved, *via lapida strata*, sanded or gravelled, *via glarea strata*, and marked track, *via terrena*. Here you can see a working party of Roman soldiers constructing a first-class road through open country. Military surveyors are using devices called *gromae* (singular *groma*), to make the line of the road straight. Bends are often put at the tops of hills, or if a descent is steep. The bed of the road is made from a layer of sand topped by layers of rubble, concrete and a surface pavement of flat stones carefully fitted together. The pavement is slightly curved so that it is higher in the middle than at the sides. This is so that rainwater can run off the road surface into the ditches at each side of the road.

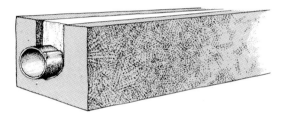

Above: Two types of clay drainpipe from the city of Ur, Mesopotamia, c3000–c2000 BC.

Above: Egyptian water conduit, c2500 BC. The pipe is made from copper sheet, folded and hammered. It is laid in channelled stone blocks, sealed with waterproof mortar.

Below: Three examples of Roman water conduits. Top to bottom: lead pipe made from lead sheet, hammered into shape and sealed with lead solder; stone pipe; sections of wooden pipe fixed together with an iron collar.

City Services

Any kind of settled community makes particular demands on the environment. There must be a constant supply of food and water, durable houses, and reliable methods of disposing of rubbish and human waste. Various centres of civilization have dealt with these problems in different ways.

The early townships of the Near East, relied on wells for their water supply. Wide pits were dug to the natural water level. Then a stone funnel was built up, course by course, back to ground level. The funnel was supported by packing the pit with the earth that had been removed to make the pit. Eventually the well was complete – a stone-lined shaft from which water could be raised by, for example, a leather bucket tied to a long rope.

Sewage

One approach to the problem of sanitation was that stone channels were laid from individual huts to a communal midden – a covered pit in which all the wastes from the community were gathered. This kind of solution was common to many early communities. In Prehistoric Skara Brae in Orkney, for example, all the houses were linked by underground tunnels. At first these were thought to be channels for rubbish disposal. It is now thought that these were access passages and that their sewage was thrown into the communal midden. But once populations grew beyond a certain point, the problem of disposal became much greater. Early evidence of city sewage systems come from ancient Babylon. Underground arched culverts were built from baked brick set in bitumen. Channels like these carried away rainwater as well as waste. They could also be flushed out by water from the canals and drainage ditches, discharging outside the city into the river. In towns and cities without proper sewage systems, waste may have been regularly collected in carts and transported to a dump beyond the city. This was certainly true in ancient China, where waste was used to fertilize the fields.

As cities grew bigger, they needed better supplies of water. The great city of Harappa (2500–1700 BC), in the Indus Valley, offered its inhabitants a number of public wells, in addition to the private wells which served individual households. In the hilltop towns of Palestine, rulers built stone conduits to carry water from constant springs to public cisterns. The Minoan palace of Knossos might have been the first building in the ancient world to have its own supply of piped running water. Sections of pottery piping have been found which may have brought water into the palace from springs some distance away.

Polycrates, ruler of the Greek island of Samos, is credited with the first attempt to bring water

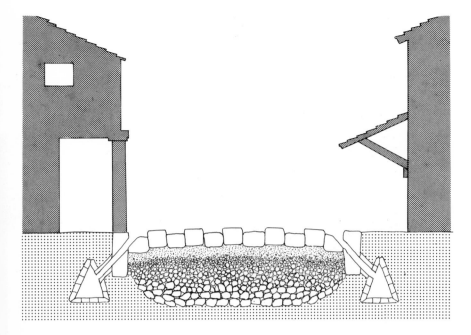

Left: Roman streets. They were built for people. Most heavy traffic was banned during the daytime. The pavements were built above the level of the road so no vehicles could accidentally roll into the path of pedestrians. The sewers were linked to the gutters so that the roads could be washed easily. Stepping stones enabled the pedestrians to cross the road without wetting their feet.

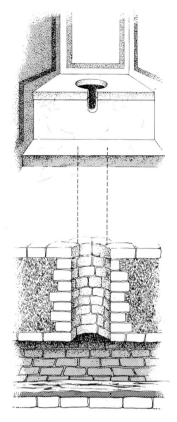

Roman water-closets were connected directly to the sewers. Imagine the smell! In a modern water closet, water in the U-bend acts as a barrier to the odours and gases.

from a distant source. He ordered a tunnel to be dug through the mountains behind his city to a lake beyond. The aqueduct was to come later, with the Romans perfecting its construction until it became a regular feature of Roman towns.

Water Supply

Roman civilization summed up and blended all the advances previously made in the ancient world. Except where local conditions and existing roads prevented it, Roman towns and cities were carefully laid out in a regular chessboard grid of paved avenues and streets. Water was piped to public fountains and private houses. Civic departments supervised the water supply, refuse collection, street cleaning and the maintenance of an excellent system of underground drains and sewers. Each town of any size had its own public baths where the furnace that heated the water also warmed the rooms through hot air vents in the walls and floors. Next to the baths were public lavatories, flushed with running water – an arrangement also common in private houses. The system of underfloor central heating used in the public baths was adapted for private

houses, especially in the colder provinces of the Roman empire.

By AD 500, Roman power in Europe was finished. Barbarian kings carved out their own territories. With the collapse of the Roman empire, trade came to a virtual standstill. The tradition of planned cities and organized government disappeared. Without order and administration, Roman towns and cities decayed or were abandoned altogether.

Slums

Once there had been laws throughout the empire to prevent houses encroaching onto the all-important highways. Now there were small localized communities in which houses were built all over the place. This made it impossible to provide effective sewage and water systems. The typical city of the Middle Ages was a slum compared to the Roman cities that had gone before. It had narrow, winding streets with open drains, tiny houses of timber and plaster rather than brick, and a primitive water supply. Centuries passed before Europe was once again strong enough to support powerful cities with well-organised city services.

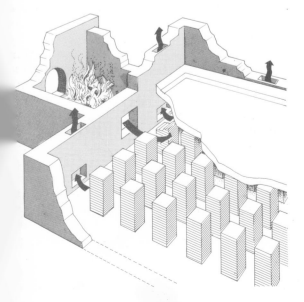

Roman central heating. The hot rooms at Roman public baths were heated by a system called a *hypocaust*. Hot air from a furnace, was directed under the floors, and also rose through hollow flues in the walls. The system was used in private houses as well.

Building a castle tower. The core of the walls is of rubble and concrete, reinforced with heavy chain. Three different types of hoist are in use, including the great wheel turned by a man walking inside it, used to haul up wooden centering for the vaulting.

Castles

During the Middle Ages, most of Europe was governed by the king and the nobility under the feudal system. Kings granted territories to their most important followers, or vassals. In return for control over a particular territory, the vassal promised to support the king and fight alongside him in time of war. This was an effective system of government at a time when the poor quality of the roads prevented a central government from directly administering the outer reaches of its territory.

A powerful feudal lord controlled his territory from a strongly built castle. When William of Normandy invaded England in 1066, the castle was his great weapon for holding on to what he had gained. The Norman motte-and-bailey castle consisted of a mount, *motte*, of earth built quickly by the Norman soldiers. But connected with a courtyard, *bailey*, surrounded by an earthen rampart and ditch. The motte-and-bailey castle was both an encampment for troops and a defensive strong-point in case of attack.

As time went on, this type of Castle was more and more strongly fortified, first with wood, then with stone. The castle mound became the foundation of the stone keep, the inner stronghold of the castle, where the lord and his family lived. The bailey, now fortified with stone walls, held living quarters for the lord's fighting men, together with facilities like stabling, workshops, a bakehouse and a blacksmith's forge.

Castles Under Siege

By the 12th century, the design of castles had become influenced by the superior fortifications that the Crusaders had come across in the Near East. The longer a castle could hold out against an attacking force, the more likely that the attackers themselves would eventually run out of food, or be overtaken by winter. Castles were designed with several walls, one inside the other. Round turrets, projecting from the walls, allowed the defenders to bombard attackers from the side as they tried to scale the walls or batter their way in. Even if the outer defences fell, the defenders could retreat to the next wall, and so on until they reached the keep.

On the left you can see a round castle tower under construction. The core of the massive wall is made from flints and rubble, bound together with mortar and reinforced with heavy iron chains. The outer casing is of stone blocks, smoothed and fitted by master stonemasons.

Under the partly completed roof, the architect discusses the progress of work with his chief assistant. They are probably themselves both master masons: all skilled craftsmen, such as stonemasons and carpenters, are paid very high wages. They may have travelled hundreds of miles to work on this particular project, which may take as long as five years to complete. In 1286, a workforce of 868 men was needed to build Harlech Castle, in Wales. Most of these, however, would have been unskilled local labourers in the service of the feudal lord.

So many castles were built that by the 14th century there was no need to build any more. The only work left to do was repairs. By the mid 17th century castles began to be dismantled as being inadequate for defence against gunpowder. The age of the great castles of Europe was at an end.

Krak des Chevaliers, a castle in Syria built by Crusaders, and influenced by advanced Muslim fortifications. The round towers gave a wide field of fire. In its heyday (12th–13th centuries AD), Krak housed some 2000 soldiers.

MOTTE-AND-BAILEY CASTLE

When the Normans invaded Britain, they had to move quickly to control the Saxon population. Duke William, now King of England, gave permission to his most powerful followers to build castles. Here you can see the type of castle that was first built – called a motte-and-bailey castle. It consisted of a wooden tower on an earth mound connected to a stockaded courtyard or bailey. A motte-and-bailey castle could be thrown up quickly within a couple weeks, using the forced labour of the local population. Such castles were sited at important points – by a river-crossing, at a cross-roads, close by a town – from which the Normans could control the district. If under attack, the Norman garrison could retreat into the castle until reinforcements arrived.

A Medieval Abbey

The finest buildings of the Middle Ages in Europe were the great abbey and cathedral churches. The Church dominated people's lives from the cradle to the grave and even, so people believed, after death. Learning and the arts were kept alive in the Church when Europe was ruled by feudal kings. People believed that the teachings of the Church were God's Word to the human race. It seemed natural to everybody, rich and poor, to give what they could to the Church to help it in its work of helping the sick and needy, preaching the Christian Gospel and praying for the souls of the departed.

From the 4th century AD, Christians who wanted to devote their lives to God began to form religious communities separate from the everyday worries of town life. These became the first monasteries. They lived according to simple rules. Individuals owned nothing, worked hard (as the communities were self-sufficient), and spent long hours in prayer. Each community lived under a particular set of rules, like the rules set down by the Italian monk St Benedict, who was born in AD 520. The Benedictines, as his followers were known, founded many communities in Europe.

These communities, some of which were known as abbeys, contained all that was needed for the religious life. The most important was the abbey church itself, where the monks held services at certain set hours each day. But there was also a dormitory where the monks slept, a library where they copied out the scriptures, the cloister, where the monks walked in silent meditation, a refectory, where they ate their meals – as well as the buildings where travellers were housed and sick persons cared for.

All the buildings in which the monks lived were as simple as possible. But the abbey church itself was built to honour God. Enormous sums of money were spent on its construction and decoration. Some churches took more than a hundred years to build. The work was paid for by the incomes and rent from church lands and by gifts from the faithful.

Before the church was begun, the head of the abbey discussed the design with a master mason who would supervise the detailed carrying out of the work. Timber and stone had to be ordered and transported to the site. Master craftsmen – stonemasons, freemasons (stone-carvers), carpenters, glassmakers, roofers and painters – had to be employed, along with armies of semi-skilled and unskilled labourers.

Styles

The first great churches of northwest Europe, such as those at Durham, England, and Cluny, France, were built in the *Romanesque* style, with round arches. The style was based on the surviving round-arched buildings of the Roman Empire. But from the 12th century the pointed 'Gothic' arch replaced the round arch in church building. The Gothic arch was the result of contact with Islamic building styles in the Near East by European pilgrims and crusaders.

The pointed 'Gothic' arch enabled church builders to replace the massively heavy Roman 'groin' vault – the extension of the round arch – with the lighter 'ribbed' vault. The load of the ribbed vaults could be taken on buttressed pillars alone (see page 9). The walls instead of having to be thickened, could be pierced with large windows without weakening the structure. The Gothic style lent itself to immensely tall churches, their interiors lit by great windows of multi-coloured stained glass.

On the left you can see stonemasons at work on the stone ribs of the vaulted ceiling of the nave, the main part of the church. The wooden lifting machine at the top of the picture has been used to lift wooden arches – centerings – into position. Stones have been laid along the centering, and a specially shaped keystone is being hoisted up to complete the arch. When it has been laid in place, and the mortar has set, the wooden centering will be taken away. The space between the stone ribs will be filled in with a light screen of stonework.

Far Left: The great lifting wheel, turned by men walking inside it, hoists up a keystone which will be lowered into position at the top of the arch. Notice the pointed arch and the windows, pierced with lancets and rosettes, of this Gothic abbey.

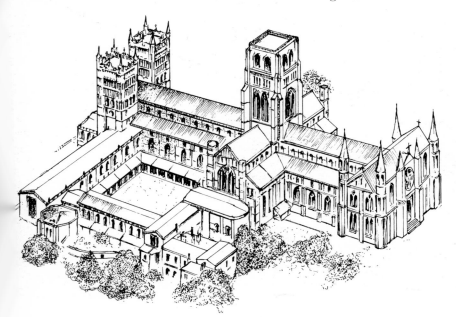

Durham Cathedral, begun in 1093, was the church of a powerful and wealthy Benedictine monastery. It is built in the pre-Gothic Anglo-Norman style. It is still surrounded by some of the original monastic buildings – the cloister court, the refectory (dining room) and the chapter or meeting house. The storehouses, guesthouse and infirmary (hospital) have been rebuilt as canons' houses. It is the first church to have ribbed vaults throughout and the earliest to use pointed arches. The massive circular columns, or piers, are decorated with bold patterns. The impression of the Romanesque interior is of overwhelming grandeur.

Monasteries fostered craftsmanship in their own workshops. Here you can see a blacksmith, a silversmith and a carpenter at work. The carpenter's brace-and-bit, and the wheelbarrow (being pushed through the door) were new to Europe in the Middle Ages.

Abbey Crafts

A Benedictine abbey aimed, as far as possible to be a self-sufficient community. For example, they had their own farms, on which the monks worked to produce the food they needed. Abbeys were also centres of craft and industry. The abbey workshops made all the articles used by the monks in their daily life. The abbey blacksmith in his forge (above) can make everything from iron nails and horseshoes to tools and farm implements: much of his time will be spent in repairing the damage caused by everyday use – a buckled ploughshare, or a broken lock on the ironbound chest that the monk is bringing in on a wheelbarrow. In the foreground, a monk shapes or 'raises' a metal bowl by beating it with a special hammer on a special anvil.

The carpenter (right) is an important crafts-man: his workshop is called upon to make wooden chairs, tables, chests, cupboards and doors. Elsewhere, there might be a pottery making the earthenware bowls and jugs used in the kitchens and at mealtimes. The carts, on which the abbey transports its produce from the fields and to market, are made by wainrights and wheelwrights.

Trade

In the 11th century, trade naturally increased in the areas around the monasteries and abbeys of Europe. Pilgrims from far away brought gift and goods to sell. The exchange of goods brought a new source of money. People rented out their houses to the monasteries in return for cultivating land that would otherwise remain derelict. The skills were available to the local people, and the surplus produce from the monastery land might be sold in exchange for articles that the monk lacked. Small towns could grow up on land belonging to a religious foundation.

Medieval Guilds

The great abbey churches of 1050–1150 began an extraordinary age of cathedral building. The difference between an abbey church and a cathedral was that the first was part of a monastery, while the second was the chief church of a particular district, or *diocese*, administered by a bishop or an archbishop. In the 12th century, for example, the Archbishop of Chartres resolved to begin a great cathedral in the new style, later known as the Gothic. Such was the enthusiasm of the citizens of Chartres that the people harnessed themselves to the carts and dragged the huge limestone blocks from the quarry to the site. The magnificent Gothic cathedrals of France and England were seen as works of faith in which everyone, rich or poor, could take pride.

As a large-scale employer of skilled craftsmen, the Church encouraged a steady advance in building techniques. Churches were built taller than ever before, and further decorated with lofty spires and towers. Inside and out, surfaces were covered with exquisitely carved stone ornaments.

All the work, from design and supervision to fine details, was carried out by craftsmen trained through the guild system. No man could work unless he belonged to his town guild, an association of fellow-craftsmen who followed the same trade. The guild fixed wages and conditions for its members. It also controlled entry in the interests of maintaining high standards of workmanship. To be accepted into a guild, an individual had first to be apprenticed for seven years to a master craftsman. At the end of this time he had to complete a particular piece of work which would satisfy the guild that he knew his job. Then he was accepted as a craftsman. In time he might become a master craftsman himself, which would make him one of the leading men in the guild.

The Masons

The most important guilds were those of the masons. The master mason was responsible for all the design and building work. Unlike other tradesmen, masons were allowed to travel away from their home town to wherever building was taking place. The various grades of mason lived and worked on the site until all the stonework was completed. Rough-masons smoothed and prepared the stone blocks from the quarry. Freemasons shaped the blocks with hammer and chisel. They were laid in place by wallers, while other masons, called imagers, carved the profusion of statuary with which the church was decorated. Masons, tilers, plasterers, carpenters worked according to the traditions of their crafts, handed down from master to apprentice.

In the Middle Ages, there was a European-wide tradition of building as a service to God and the church. For a craftsman, glory lay in the knowledge that he had satisfactorily completed an offering to God. This lack of vanity is one of the reasons why we know very few of the names of the thousands of craftsmen who toiled on the churches of the Middle Ages.

The craftsmen employed to work on the churches of the Middle Ages belonged to organizations called guilds, each devoted to a particular trade. Entry to the guilds was carefully controlled.

Below: A section through a Gothic church, showing how the structure was supported, or buttressed.

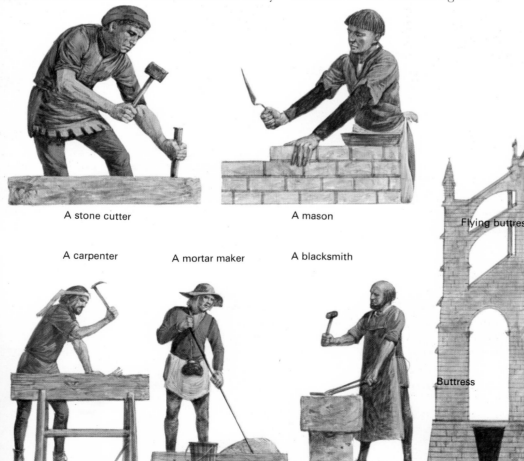

A stone cutter

A mason

A carpenter

A mortar maker

A blacksmith

Flying buttress

Buttress

Cutaway view of the dome designed for Florence Cathedral by the architect Brunelleschi. The pointed dome, some 42 metres in diameter, blends the Gothic with the new classical style of the Renaissance. The government in Florence wanted to build a cathedral that would outshine the great cathedrals of Siena and Pisa. Unfortunately the tower was built so large that using conventional methods no dome could be built to cover it. Filippo Brunelleschi solved the problem. Brunelleschi also invented a special crane with which to build the lantern. A frame enabled the builders to run a series of pulleys which moved the stone blocks laterally as well as vertically. The lateral pulley system was counterbalanced with a large weight.

1. Brunelleschi's crane
2. Lantern
3. Main ribs
4. Minor ribs
5. Horizontal ribs
6. Octagonal drum
7. Circular windows

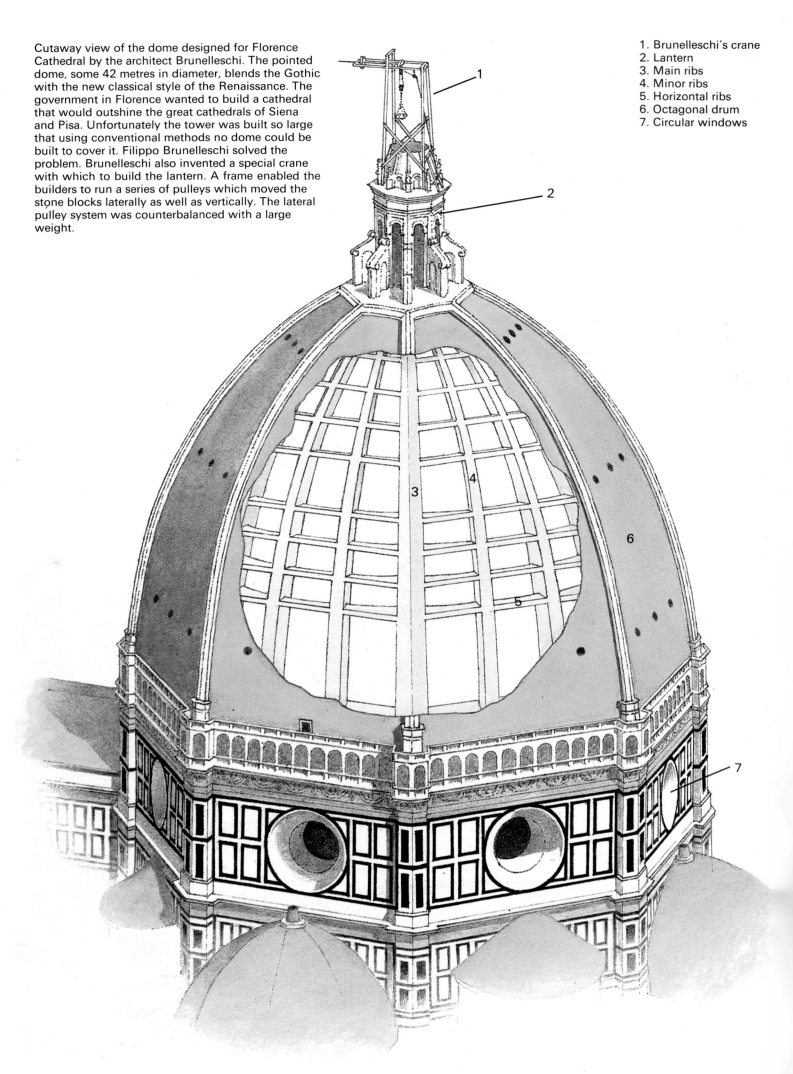

a huge mountain: the many stages of the pagoda represented all the myriad levels of the Earth-mountain. The Chinese believed that the pagoda, with the precious relics within, would help them to harmonize their actions on Earth with the Will of Heaven.

Spires

From the 11th century AD, the church builders of Europe began to construct very tall towers, often crowned with delicately tapering spires. This must have been very dangerous work. Above a certain height it was no longer possible to build firm scaffolding. Men worked on platforms built out from the walls. The timbers, called putlogs, were set into special holes left in the wall: they supported platforms of wickerwork rather than the scaffolding planks used today. Even more hair-raising must have been the wickerwork cradles, raised and lowered by a hoist, shown in drawings and paintings of the time.

Above: The Pharos at Alexandria, some 135 metres high, was a lighthouse famous as one of the tallest buildings in the world. Pharos was a small island in the bay of Alexandria about a mile from the mainland. Dexiphanes built a causeway linking the two in 284 BC. It was on this causeway that the lighthouse was built by Sostratus, the son of Dexiphanes. It was considered to be one of the seven wonders of the world, was built with white marble and its light could be seen at a distance of 200 kilometres. Because the bay was dangerous, fires were kept burning constantly on the top by sailors of the Egyptian navy. The building of the tower was enormously expensive and the king at the time, Ptolemy II, wanted the glory for it, so had inscribed on the building: *King Ptolemy to the Gods the saviours, for the benefit of sailors.* But after some time the mortar wore away and revealed, was the following inscription: *Sostratus, the Cnidian, son of Dexiphanes, to the Gods the saviours, for the benefit of sailors.*

Below: The Ince Minare mosque at Konya, in Turkey, was built between 1258 and 1262 AD. The name means 'slender minaret'. The minaret was connected to the mosque and was originally twice as tall as it now stands – an earthquake caused the other half to fall. All minarets had a balcony from which a *muezzin* – a Muslim crier – calls the hours of prayer. The tallest minaret is in Delhi, India built in 1194 to a height of 72 metres.

By 500 AD, Buddhist teachings had reached all parts of China from India. The Chinese had seen the ever more elaborate Indian *stupas* – the sacred Indian Buddhist domed temples. The Indian temple at Shah-ji-ki-Dheri was the most elaborate. So impressed were the Chinese that they built a pagoda in imitation of the spire of the stupa alone. Pagodas like this were built as part of Buddhist temples and monasteries. The many storeys of the pagodas symbolized the great variety of life on Earth. The tallest pagoda is at Rangoon, Burma and is 100 metres high, built in 1763. The oldest is in Honan, China and was built with fifteen 12-sided storeys in AD 523.

Tools

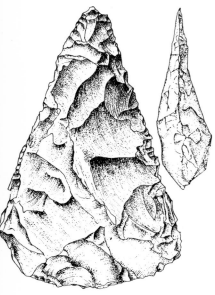

Above: 1. Stone Axe 400,000 years old.

Below: 2. Stone-bladed tools. Left to right: axe, adze or pick, sickle, all about 6000 BC.

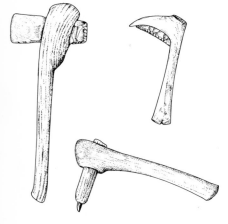

Below: 3. Bow drill with flint bit, Egypt c2000 BC

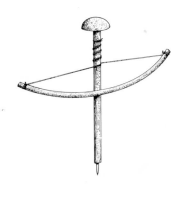

Humans are not the only animals to use tools. Chimpanzees have been observed using sticks to get at objects out of their reach. But humans are the only animals to adapt and alter natural materials for a particular function. Tools are divided into three main classes: tools that move things, such as the lever and tongs; tools that shape things, such as axes, hammers and chisels; and tools that mark or measure.

1. Stone Axe

Hand tools were being made in East Africa more than 400,000 years ago, and in Europe more than 200,000 years ago. This one has been made from the core of a flint, shaped by removing flakes of material from the outside, using a hammer stone.

2. Neolithic (New Stone Age) Tools

Early farmers in Europe used stone tools such as these after 5000 BC. On the left, the polished stone axe was efficient for felling trees to clear the land. The axe-head was smoothed and polished to give it greater penetration or 'bite'. The wooden handle gave more leverage, and therefore more power when the axe was swung. In the centre is a flint-bladed adze. Before the development of the metal chisel, the adze was the traditional carpenter's tool. With it, Stone Age builders were able to shape timber very skilfully. Here the flint blade has been socketed into a deer antler. On the right is a flint-bladed sickle for cutting down crops. The haft is a curved animal bone: the blade is a series of small flakes of flint set in resin.

3. Drills

Two types of drill are shown here. The carpenter's bow drill works by moving the bow backwards and forwards. This makes it spin clockwise and anticlockwise. In use, the top of the spindle is steadied by fitting it loosely into a mushroom-shaped stone socket held in the worker's free hand. The mason's spin drill works by being spun between the palms of the hands: the weights at the top of the spindle help the worker to spin the drill more steadily and powerfully. Drills like these were used to bore holes in stone. Both the bow drill and spin drill have flint 'bits' which can be replaced if they chip or shatter.

4. Metal Tools

Tools like the copper axe and copper chisel were expensive and were not necessarily more efficient than stone tools. They are not as hard as stone tools. But broken metal tools could be re-used by melting them down and re-casting them into any shape.

5. Saws

The earliest metal saws were curved bronze blades with a series of notches cut in them. Egyptian paintings show a carpenter sawing

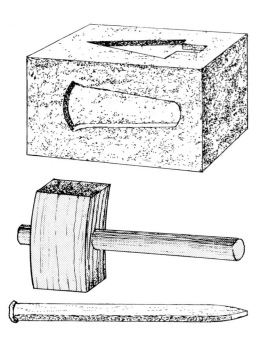

4. Stone mould for copper axe-head, c3000 BC (top). Copper chisels and mallet, c2500 BC (bottom).

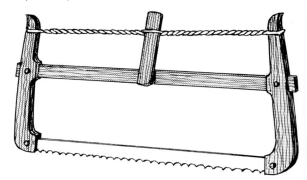

5. Saw with bronze blade.

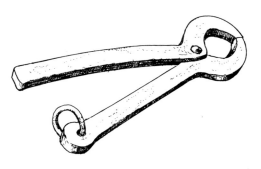

6. Metalworker's tongs, c500 BC.

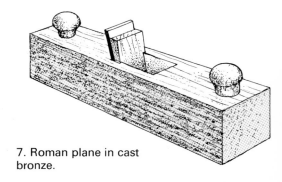

7. Roman plane in cast bronze.

9. Boning rods.

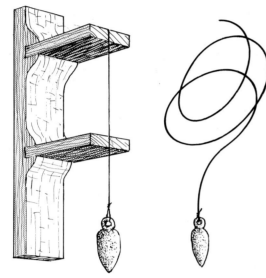

10. Plumb line, Plumb rule.

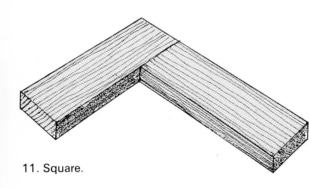

11. Square.

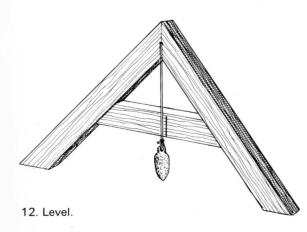

12. Level.

trees into planks with the wood held vertically, while his assistant keeps the cut open by easing the plank away from the main piece of wood.

6. Tongs

Hinged metal tongs were used after 1100 BC by metalworkers. They were used by blacksmiths to hold the red hot iron as it was hammered on the anvil.

7. Plane

The plane was a Roman invention. Until then, carpenters used the adze for squaring timber, which was then smoothed by rubbing with an abrasive material, such as sand. The plane allowed the carpenter to smooth timber more quickly. The basic design and shape of the plane has scarcely altered in nearly 2000 years.

8. Snap Line

The stonemason needed a method of marking and squaring the stone that he was about to cut. The snap line is a simple and effective marker. The line is covered with powdered chalk, and stretched tightly across the face of the work. When the line is 'snapped' – pulled away from the work, then released – it leaves a straight chalk mark on the stone along its length. The same method was also used to mark up timber.

9. Boning Rods

These straight pieces of wood were used to check the smoothness of the work in progress. For example, early stonemasons shaped stone blocks both by pounding with balls of hard stone, and by smoothing with flat stones and sand. At various stages in this process the boning rods were set against the stone faces to check how much more stone had to be removed before the block was completely smooth.

10. Plumb Line, Plumb Rule

A plumb line is a weighted line which, when allowed to hang freely, is truly vertical. It is the simplest accurate measuring tool. In a plumb rule, the plumb line is contained in a wooden frame, so as to measure the 'true' of vertical walls, for example. Both were used by the early builders of Mesopotamia and Egypt.

11. Square

The square is an L-shaped piece in which the two inner sides are exactly at right angles to one another. Masons used the square to check that the faces of stone blocks were at right angles to one another.

12. Level

The level shown here is a combination of square and plumb line used to find a true horizontal. It was in common use in ancient Egypt.

13. Auger

Adaptation of the simple screw first used by the Greeks to make holes in wood.

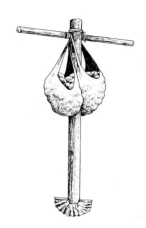

(top). Mason's drill, operated by spinning between the palms, Egyptian c2000 BC. It bores bigger holes (bottom).

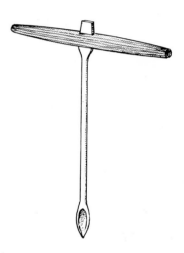

13. Auger. Tool for piercing holes in wood.

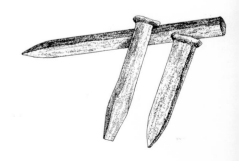

45609

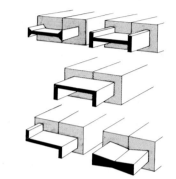

The wattle fences were threaded. Strategic holes were drilled and the fence poles secured in them. Then the whole structure was daubed in mud and plastered over. From prehistoric times to the Middle Ages, wattle-and-daub was a major building material in Europe.

Different sorts of metal joints used by the Greeks to hold lengths of stone together.

Mudbrick. Clay mixed with water and chopped straw, formed in a wooden mould and turned out to dry in the sun.

Below: Techniques used to work stone. A. Splitting rock by driving wooden wedges into a natural or man-made crack. When soaked with water, the wood expands, forcing the rock apart. B. Pounding with a very hard stone. Balls of dolerite were used by Egyptian masons. C. Chiselling. Earliest chisels were of copper, later of bronze, then of iron or steel

Technology

Weaving and Thatching

Weaving and plaiting vegetable fibres are among the oldest human skills. Early peoples knotted fibres into fishing nets, wove them into baskets, or plaited them into simple, temporary shelters. These skills were adapted to play a vital part in the history of building. Wattle, for example, is a type of basketwork made of split cane woven in and out of upright stakes. In Europe, especially, wattle coated with mud plaster (daub), was used for house walls from about 6000 BC until the 17th century AD. Thatch – overlapping bundles of straw or reeds – was a roofing material generally used throughout the same period. In Mesopotamia, there was an unlimited supply of reeds (growing up to 4 metres tall). Early dwellings were made from bundles of reeds lashed together and covered with woven reed matting. Later, woven reed baskets were used to carry the clay used to make mudbrick. Boats, of reed matting covered in waterproof bitumen, or of bundles of reeds tied together, transported building materials by water.

Fastenings

Any building involves fixing materials together. Early techniques included sewing with bone needles and 'thread' of animal sinew (string-like tissue connecting muscle to bone). Tents, for example, were made by sewing together a number of animal hides. Timbers were lashed with twine or rope made from vegetable fibres or animal hair. Natural glues were made from beeswax, and resinous gums which came from certain trees and plants. In ancient Egypt, carpenters used a glue made from boiling down animal skin, bone and sinews. Mesopotamian craftsmen could call on bitumen, a natural tar which, soft when warmed, set hard on cooling. Before nails of hard bronze and iron were available, timbers were sometimes fixed together with wooden pegs or dowels. Metals were riveted, that is joined with small metal pegs, then the top and bottom of the peg were flattened out by hammering. Brick and stone were jointed by a variety of adhesive mortars. The simplest of these was clay mixed with water. Much tougher mortars were made by burning gypsum and limestone, mixing the powder with water, then mixing the putty-like result with sand and water. In Roman times an extremely hard concrete was made from a mixture of lime, sand, volcanic ash and water.

Brickmaking

The great building material of the Near East was river clay. When puddled with water, mixed with straw and animal hair, it could be formed into bricks by drying naturally in the sun. Early mudbricks were formed by hand, but at some point wooden moulds were introduced to make bricks of a standard size. Bricks like these were used for houses in Egypt and Mesopotamia, for the cores of large monumental buildings like temples and palaces. The disadvantage of sun-dried brick was that, in time, it crumbled away to dust or was washed away by water. If clay brick is fired (burned in a kiln), however, it lasts much longer. Kiln baked bricks were first made in Mesopotamia from about 3500 BC. But the process was expensive and burned bricks were used only for special purposes like decorative facing, and for waterproof foundations and canal linings. Not until Roman times were fired bricks mass-produced for general building purposes.

Stoneworking

At first sight, it is difficult to believe that ancient peoples worked stone without metal tools. But, using a variety of techniques, they were able to produce work of astonishing accuracy. Stone could be quarried by forcing wooden wedges into natural cracks in the rock. When soaked with water, the wooden wedges expanded, splitting a slab of rock away from the face. Another method was to set a fire against the rockface: the heat of the fire caused the stone to crack and fall away. Rough blocks could be shaped by pounding with a very hard stone, like the balls of dolerite used by Egyptian masons. They could be smoothed and polished by rubbing with a flat stone, using sand as an abrasive. Squares, boning rods and plumb lines were used to check that the work was perfectly square and smooth (see Tools). The introduction of copper, and later bronze, tools may have made stoneworking less laborious, but did not change the basic techniques. Long before then, for example, stone was drilled with a flint-tipped spin drill. It was even possible to drill holes through stone using a hollow bone. The bone was spun back and forth between the palms, while the end in contact with the stone was fed with sand. Gradually the bone drilled out a cylindrical 'plug'.

Rammed Earth and Cob

In ancient China, walls were made of rammed earth rather than mudbrick or wattle-and-daub. The earth was shovelled into large rectangular wooden frames and stamped down until firm. Then the frame was dismantled, a new layer of rammed earth built on top of the first and so on. The outside face of the wall was plastered with a mixture of lime, earth and water which, when dry, protected the wall from the weather. In some parts of Europe, too, rammed earth was used for walls. One type, called cob, was a mixture of chalk, earth and cow dung.

Surveying

Today, very accurate instruments are used to survey land – that is, to measure distance, area and rise and fall. In the ancient world, however, only very simple instruments were available. In Egypt and Mesopotamia, rods and lines of fixed lengths were used to measure fields for tax purposes. The need to build canals and ditches led to an understanding of how water-levels could show the rise and fall of land. The unchanging pattern of life allowed methods of measurement to develop over generations to a high degree of accuracy. The Romans on the other hand were an expanding people imposing their civilization on new lands. They used an instrument called a *groma*, with which they could divide up conquered territory in squares of fixed area. The *chorobalt*, a crude spirit-level in the form of a trough filled with water, was adopted by the Romans as a method of fixing the angle of slope needed for aqueducts.

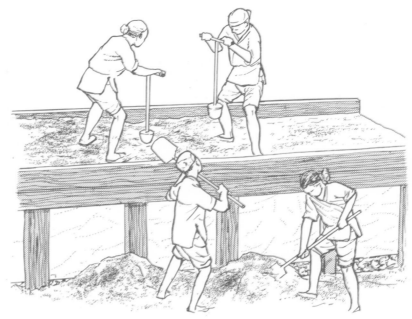

Above: A tamped or rammed earth wall under construction. Wooden shuttering is made rigid. Dry earth is rammed inside until solid. The shuttering is then removed and the process repeated at a higher level. Bamboo was sometimes placed between the layers to absorb moisture.

Roman surveyors using a *groma*, a device for laying out right angles. The surveyor looks along the metal rule and lines up the man holding the piece of string. The string is secured at both ends. He then repeats the process along the other metal rule. The plumb lines are to ensure that the metal rules are in the same plane.

Power

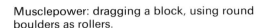

Steam power was first harnessed in the 18th century AD. Until then, human beings relied for their power on draught animals, human muscle, fire, and the natural energy from the sun, wind and water.

Wherever the land could feed large, settled populations, there was a pool of labour which could be employed in the fields for part of the year. As long as human musclepower was available on a large scale, labour-saving machines were not needed.

The ox was the first animal to be harnessed to work for human beings. The earliest type of harness, the yoke, was attached to the horns of the oxen. The horse, native to central Asia, was introduced into the Near East about 1500 BC. But the horse was not suited to hauling heavy loads. The type of harness then used pressed against the animal's windpipe, affecting its breathing, and so cutting down the amount of work it could do. The Romans worked out that a horse could do 4 times the work of a man, but ate 4 times as much as a slave. On balance, then, there was no reason to replace human muscle power with horse power.

Fire was the most effective way of altering raw materials so as to make them more useful to human beings. By about 4000 BC the pottery kiln was in use in Mesopotamia. It was a dome-shaped oven, with an opening at the base and a vent in the top. The inside was divided into an upper and a lower compartment by a shelf of baked clay, which was pierced by a series of holes. The lower compartment held the fuel (reeds) while the pottery was piled on the shelf above. The draught through the kiln made the fire burn at a higher temperature. Kilns like these were later used to make fired bricks and glazed bricks which were used to decorate the temples and palaces of Mesopotamia. The high temperatures needed to melt copper from its ore were produced by blowing the fire with long reed blowpipes. After 2000 BC, the use of bellows (perhaps introduced from central Asia) made it easier and quicker for metals to be worked on a

Sun-dried mudbrick from Jericho, Palestine, c5000 BC. The ridges were made so that the mud mortar could bind to the brick.

THE WHEEL

Our first knowledge of the wheel comes from Mesopotamia, where two-wheeled carts and four-wheeled wagons appeared in about 3500 BC. The wheels were made in three parts from a single plank of hard wood cut from the heart of a tree trunk (1). By 1500 BC the two-wheeled horse drawn chariot was in use in the Near East. This was a fast, manoeuverable weapon of war. Accordingly the wheels were lightened by making them spoked rather than solid. Hard dense timber was used for the hubs: a strong, straight timber made up the spokes. The outer circle, or felloe, was made from a wood, like ash, which could be softened and bent by heat (2). From 1300 BC, chariot wheels were made with eight or more spokes and heavier felloes, perhaps for travelling over rougher ground (3). Leonardo da Vinci designed the flared wheel (4) in the 15th century in Italy.

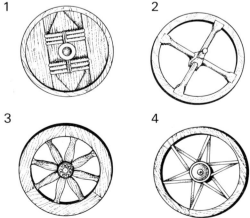

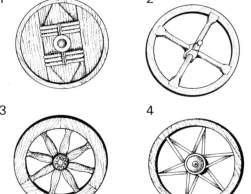

Musclepower: dragging a block, using round boulders as rollers.

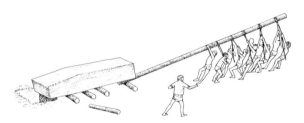

Above: In Egypt, heavy blocks were dragged on wooden sleds along wooden causeways: the runners of the sleds were 'lubricated' with sand to make them run more smoothly.

Above: The lever is the simplest of machines: it allows human beings to concentrate their efforts on moving a heavy weight a small distance at a time. Here, a gang uses a lever and rollers to manoeuvre a heavy stone into a prepared hole.

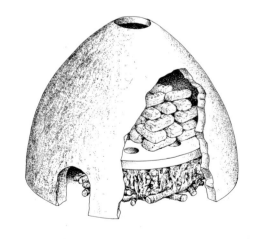

Above: The development of the pottery kiln in about 4000 BC was a new stage in the control of fire. Kiln baked bricks came to be used for decoration and for waterproof channels and foundations. High-temperature furnaces, for smelting copper, came into use by 3000 BC.

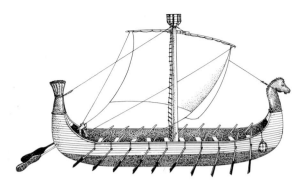

Above: Phoenician merchant ship of the 10th century BC. Sailing craft first appeared in Mesopotamia and Egypt before 3000 BC. Transport by water was always cheaper than overland transport.

Above: The *shaduf*: this simple device for lifting water was in use in Egypt by 2000 BC.

much larger scale.

In the Near East, the power of the Sun enabled farming peoples to build substantial houses, towns and cities from sun-dried clay bricks. Mudbrick, to give it its proper name, has remained an important building material in the Near East and Middle East to the present day.

Wind provided the power for sailing craft which first sailed to Egypt and Mesopotamia before 3000 BC. Transport by water was always cheaper and more effective than land transport.

Machines

Machines are devices which channel sources of power to perform particular tasks more effectively. Until Greek and Roman times very few machines existed. The simplest were the lever, for moving heavy weights, and the wedge, used for example to split rock into blocks. The Greeks may have been the first to use hoists in which a rope was passed over a pulley wheel. The rope could be hauled by hand or wound round a cylindrical drum turned by projecting levers – a windlass. The Romans adapted the windlass by attaching a 'mouse-wheel' to it: the large hollow wheel was fixed to the winding drum of the hoist. One or two men walking inside the wheel turned it. The Romans also developed the wheel powered by running water for grinding corn and pumping water from mines.

Watermills, and later windmills, were used to drive the bellows and hammers used in metalworking. Wheelbarrows, were invented by the Chinese in the 3rd century AD, although they were unknown in Europe until the 14th century. They were an important advance, enabling one man to do the work of two.

Right: The Romans adapted a type of Greek hoist to make a crane. They fixed a treadmill to the winding drum: it was turned by one or more persons walking on the spot inside the hollow treadmill.

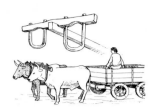

Above: Shoulder harness used in ox-drawn vehicles. The same type was much less effective when used to harness horses. The ox remained the main draught animals of ancient times.

Above: The wheelbarrow was invented in China in the 3rd century AD.

Below: The lathe – a machine for shaping wood or stone by spinning it against a stationary tool – was in use by the 3rd century BC.

Above: The watermill was developed by the Romans in the 1st century AD. In this type, called the undershot mill, the paddle-wheel was turned from below by the natural flow of a river or stream. The Romans used watermills chiefly for grinding corn: in China, however, water power was employed in making and forging metals.

73

MEASUREMENTS IN THE ANCIENT WORLD

Average height = 4 cubits

Cubit = 1 unit

Foot = $\frac{2}{3}$ unit

Great span = $\frac{1}{2}$ unit

Little span = $\frac{1}{3}$ unit

Long palm = $\frac{1}{6}$ unit

Short palm = $\frac{1}{7}$ unit

Digit = $\frac{1}{24}$ unit

Measurements in the ancient world were based on the relationships between different parts of the body. The basic unit was the cubit – the distance between a man's elbow and his fingertips. Although the length of the cubit varied from place to place, the proportions between the measurements stayed very much the same.

Average height of a man = 4 cubits
1 cubit = 6 palms = 24 digits
1 foot = $\frac{2}{3}$ cubit

Egypt
Royal cubit = 6 palms = 524 mm   5 mm
1 palm = 4 digits = 87mm
1 digit = 22mm

Sumer
1 cubit = 495 mm
1 foot = $\frac{2}{3}$ cubit = 330 mm

Assyria
1 cubit = 549mm

Greece
1 cubit = 527 mm
1 Greek foot = 316 mm

Rome
1 Roman foot = 16 digits = 296 mm

England
1 English foot = 335 mm
1 rod or perch = 15 feet
1 furlong = 600 feet

Glossary

ACHAEANS   Greek-speaking inhabitants of mainland Greece during the Bronze Age in the Aegean (c2000–1200 BC). Achaean kings ruled from citadels at Mycenae and Tiryns.

AKKAD   A region in central Mesopotamia at one time controlled by Sargon the Great, king of the city of Akkad. After 1800 BC, Akkad and Sumer were absorbed into Babylonia.

ANATOLIA   The western part of the modern state of Turkey. Also called Asia Minor, Anatolia is a peninsula, with the Black Sea to the north, the Aegean Sea to the west and the Mediterranean to the south.

ARCADE   A series of arches. Roman aqueducts took advantage of the fact that an arcade need be buttressed only at each end.

ASSYRIA   The area of northern Mesopotamia controlled intermittently by a people originating near the city of Ashur.

BABYLONIA   The region of southern Mesopotamia originally controlled by Hammurabi (c1955–1913 BC) of Babylon, a city on the Euphrates river.

BITUMEN   A natural tar, associated with the oil reserves of the Middle East, found in various forms from solid to semi-liquid. Bitumen was used to waterproof reed boats and also as a waterproof mortar for foundations and canal linings.

BRONZE   A general name for various mixtures, or alloys, of copper and other metals, such as tin, zinc, lead and silver. Bronze melts at a lower temperature than copper, and is also a harder metal. These qualities made it more suitable than copper for tools and weapons.

BUTTRESS   Any part of a building that has been specially strengthened to support the structure as a whole.

CARYATID   A stone female figure, originally used in certain Greek temples as a support for masonry.

CELLA   The small, inner chamber of a Greek or Roman temple.

COFFERING   A technique developed by the Romans to lighten the weight of a dome. Square, box-like openings – coffers – were left in the underside of the dome. Arranged in patterns, coffering became an ornamental as well as a structural feature.

CONCRETE   A mixture of cement, sand and water together with gravel or crushed stone. When dry, concrete sets rock-hard. The Romans made skilled use of concrete in a wide variety of building operations: arches, domes, walls, were all concstructed largely of concrete.

CYCLOPEAN MASONRY   Large, irregular blocks of stone fitted together without mortar. The term derives from Cyclops, a one-eyed giant of Greek Mythology. Iron Age Greeks believed that the massive fortifications of the Bronze Age Achaeans could only have been built by such giants!

DOLERITE An extremely hard volcanic rock, sometimes called 'black granite', used by early Egyptian stonemasons to shape and fashion limestone blocks.

DROMOS The passageway leading to the ceremonial entrance of a Mycenean tholos (beehive) tomb.

FEUDAL SYSTEM A type of government in which a ruler rewards his followers with grants of land in return for their armed assistance in time of war.

FLYING BUTTRESS A supporting arch which leads the weight of a building to a free-standing buttress. In Gothic architecture, flying buttresses enabled exceptionally tall buildings to be constructed.

FRESCO A method of applying paint to fresh plaster so that when the plaster dries out, the paint is permanently locked into the plaster. Some frescoes have survived for thousands of years.

GOTHIC The name given to a style of architecture which developed first in France, then in England from about AD 1150. Gothic churches were built with lofty interiors in the form of a tall pointed arch, a shape which was also used for windows. Notre Dame in Paris and Salisbury Cathedral in England are examples of Gothic architecture.

INDUS VALLEY A large, fertile region in Pakistan, to the north-west of the modern state of India. Between about 2500 and 1750 BC, cities and towns were built, supported by large scale farming.

IRAN A vast region, some of which is now occupied by the state of Iran, which connects Mesopotamia with the sub-continent of India. In ancient times Iran was part of a great empire ruled by Persian kings.

LATHE A device by which a craftsman can spin his work round in order to shape it more effectively. Lathes were first used in Egypt during the 3rd century BC.

LIME A chemical produced by, for example, burning limestone to a powder, then adding water to it, forming a lime putty. Mixed with sand and water, lime eventually dries hard. Lime was used in the ancient world to make a wide range of plasters, mortars and concretes. It is still used today for the same purpose.

MAYA An Amerindian people of Central America. From about 500 BC to AD 900, the Maya developed a way of life in which religion, astronomy, the calculation of accurate calendars, and the building of great ceremonial centres and temples, were brought to a high level.

MEGALITH A word based on two Greek words meaning 'great stone'. Prehistoric standing stones, and stone circles like Stonehenge are often described as 'megalithic' monuments.

MEGARON A type of house which established itself in mainland Greece in very early times. Its ground-plan consisted of two rooms: a small antechamber leading into a larger room. The plan of later temples in Classical Greece was based on the megaron.

MINOAN The name given to the Bronze Age civilization of Crete which ended in about 1450 BC. The word refers back to a legendary king of Crete, Minos, who appears in Greek myths of the 6th century BC.

MOTTE-AND-BAILEY CASTLE A temporary fortification, consisted of an earth mound (motte) connected to a walled courtyard (bailey). Motte-and-bailey castles were built by the Normans during their conquest of England in AD 1066.

MUDBRICK Sun dried bricks made of river clay mixed with water and chopped straw or animal dung. Mudbrick was the universal building material in the Middle East by about 4000 BC.

MYCENAEANS The Achaean inhabitants of Mycenae in mainland Greece. It was at Mycenae that the first discoveries were made which proved the existence of a Bronze Age Greek civilization, from about 1600–1150 BC.

ORE Metalbearing rock. The greater the proportion of metal, the purer the ore.

PENDENTIVE Curved, triangular pieces of masonry used to support a circular dome above a square opening.

PHOENICIANS A people who lived in coastal cities in what is now the Lebanon. Seafarers, traders and craftsmen, the Phoenicians founded new cities around the Mediterranean including Cadiz in Spain, and Carthage in north Africa.

PLASTER Any coating which, applied wet, dries to a hard finish. Plasters made from clay and water, and from lime and water, were in common use in the ancient world.

POLIS A Greek word used to refer to the independent city-states which grew up in the Greek world after 800 BC.

POST-AND-LINTEL CONSTRUCTION A building method in which vertical posts or columns support horizontal lintels or beams.

RENAISSANCE The term often used to describe a revival of interest in ancient Roman and Greek language and art. This revival began in northern Italy in the 14th century and led to new fashions in literature, art and architecture.

STUCCO A weatherproof plaster applied to surfaces exposed to the open air.

SUMER The ancient name for the southern region of Mesopotamia where the first cities were built by about 3500 BC. After 2000 BC Sumer became known as Babylonia.

TOU-KUNG CONSTRUCTION The Chinese method of post-and-lintel construction. The posts were topped with spreading, branched pieces which supported horizontal beams and rafters.

VAULT A structure which covers, or spans, an area. Roman vaults were tunnel shaped. Gothic vaults were in the shape of tall, pointed arches.

VOUSSOIR A wedge-shaped brick or stone block which, with others, goes to form a semi-circular arch.

WINDLASS A winding drum to which spokes are attached in order to make it easier to turn. The Greeks used windlasses as part of a rope and pulley hoist – a means of raising heavy timbers and stone blocks.

Index

BC	EUROPE	NEAR & MIDDLE EAST
15000	In eastern Europe, hunters live in skin tents anchored by mammoth bones. In western Europe, cave-dwellings are in use.	In Iraq and Iran hunter-gatherers live in reed huts. In the Near East (Anatolia and Palestine) campsites are occupied on a semi-permanent basis. In Palestine, food gatherers and herders build round, domed huts of stone and mud.
6000		Large farming communities live in townships like Catal Hüyük in Anatolia (Turkey) and Jericho in Palestine. Houses are made from bricks of sun-dried mud. In southern Mesopotamia farming is carried on by artificial irrigation. The development of farming in the Near East leads to the growth of permanent villages.
4000	European farmers live in thatched long-houses made from wattle-and-daub In Portugal and France, peoples bury their dead in tombs constructed from large stones.	Farming villages are established in the Nile valley. Mudbrick temples are built in southern Mesopotamia. In Egypt, unified under kings from c3100 BC, stone is used to build huge pyramids in which the bodies of Egyptian kings are buried.
2000	In the island of Crete, seafaring traders and farmers are ruled from large, unfortified palaces. In Britain, work on the great stone monument of Stonehenge continues over several hundred years. Bronze-working spreads slowly westwards across Europe.	Hammurabi rules Mesopotamia from his capital, Babylon. From now on, southern Mesopotamia is known as Babylonia. The horse-drawn chariot is introduced by peoples from the steppes of Asia. Egypt is controlled by chariot-using invaders, the Hyksos.
1500	At sites in mainland Greece, Greek-speaking peoples build fortified citadels and bury the bodies of kings and aristocrats in rich graves like the Treasury of Atreus at Mycenae.	
	During a period of raids and invasions, most centres in Greece and Crete are destroyed.	The New Kingdom of Egypt becomes very powerful. Many new temples are built, especially at Luxor and Karnak. Ironworking is carried on in Anatolia. In Palestine, David establishes a Jewish kingdom with its capital at Jerusalem. His son, Solomon, expands the power of Israel, founding many new cities and building the Temple. Assyrian kings build great palaces. Nebuchadnezzar II of Babylon comes to rule all the former Assyrian possessions.
1000	Ironworking, established in middle Europe, begins to spread westwards. Greeks found colonies and trading stations from Spain to the Black Sea.	
500	Greece is threatened by the expanding Persian Empire. Under the leadership of Pericles, the Athenians build a magnificent new temple, the Parthenon. Alexander the Great, leads a united Greek force in the conquest of the Persian Empire. Alexander's empire is broken up into independent Greek-ruled kingdoms.	Near East and Middle East is divided into Greek ruled kingdoms. These are eventually absorbed into the Roman empire.
AD	The Celtic peoples of Europe are ruled by chieftains based in fortified hill towns. The Romans rise to become the strongest power in Italy. Under the emperors, Roman power extends as far as the Scottish border.	
500	The Vikings of Scandinavia establish colonies in Britain, Ireland, France and Sicily.	Rome's empire in the East survives the fall of the western empire. It is ruled from Constantinople (Byzantium), now a major centre of Christianity.
1000	The Norman descendants of Viking conquerors seize the throne of England under William, Duke of Normandy. They control the Saxon population from fortified castles.	
	At places like Durham, in England, and Cluny, in France, monks supervise the building of splendid churches. There follows a great age of church building in a new style — Gothic.	Constantinople (Byzantium) is captured by Islamic Ottoman Turks, becoming the capital of the Ottoman empire.
1500	In wealthy Tuscany there is a revival of interest in the literature, art and architecture of ancient Rome, typified by the round arch, fluted columns and the dome.	

FAR EAST

OTHER AREAS

In America and Australia, hunting peoples occupy cave dwellings.
Hunters reach the southern tip of South America. Caves and temporary shelters are in use.

15000

6000

In China, farmers live in villages of timber and thatch dwellings.

4000

Farming is carried on in the Indus Valley.

Farming begins in north east Mexico.

Towns and cities grow up in the Indus Valley. At Mohenjo-Daro and Harappa, large mudbrick granaries are built to store surplus grain.

Farming villages grow up in central America.

2000

The Indus valley civilization disappears during a period of invasions from Iran.

1500

Bronze-working begins in China. The two-wheeled horse-drawn chariot is in use. The Chou dynasty of kings expand their power over a wide area.

The valley of the Hwang-ho river in China is ruled by the Shang dynasty of kings, which is later displaced by the Chou dynasty. Chinese writing develops.
Buddhism becomes established in India.

1000

After nearly three centuries of war between rival Chinese states, the state of Ch'in emerges victorious. The Ch'in Emperor, Shi Huang-ti, unites all China under his rule. He completes the building of the Great Wall, a defence against raids by mounted nomads of the Asian steppes.

The first ceremonial centres are built in Peru.
Temples in mudbrick and stone are being built in Central and South America. The buildings are often raised on great platforms or pyramids.

500

In India, the Buddhist emperor Asoka rules a vast empire.

Under the emperor Wu Ti, Chinese armies reach northern Vietnam.

AD

Buddhist missionaries carry the Buddhist way of life to China.
Buddhist temples and pagodas are built in China.

The Maya people of Mexico build new temples and platforms in stone. At Teotihuacan an enormous temple city is built and enlarged over several hundred years.

The Toltecs create an empire in the Valley of Mexico.

500

In Africa, the Acropolis of Zimbabwe is being built in the east. In the west, Ghana is growing into a powerful empire.

1000

Mongols of central Asia begin a career of conquest and invasion under the leadership of Genghis Khan, threatening Europe, Mesopotamia, India and occupying China.

The Aztecs of Mexico rule an empire from their capital at Tenochtitlan (Mexico City). Later, the Incas establish their empire in Peru.

1500